CHARISMA

How to get
"that special magic"

Marcia Grad
Foreword by Melvin Powers

Melvin Powers
Wilshire Book Company
12015 Sherman Road
North Hollywood, California 91605

Printed in the United States of America
Library of Congress Catalog Card Number: 86-61895
ISBN 0-87980-418-1

DEDICATION

To those individuals throughout the years whose unique perceptions of life clarified my vision of it and to all the authors, students, and clients who helped to shape the Charisma Development Program by sharing with me their experiences as they evolved into the persons they had dreamed of becoming.

ACKNOWLEDGMENTS

Special appreciation to my daughter, Laura, the original product of my philosophies, whom I both taught and learned from as we shared and grew and matured together.

My deepest gratitude to Carole Foley for her insightful suggestions and irreplaceable friendship.

My heartfelt thanks to Melvin Powers, my publisher and friend, for his continuous support and expert guidance, and to Karnie Starrett for her editorial expertise and winning smile.

Foreword

Can you really get "that special magic"? Emphatically, "Yes!" says Marcia Grad, author of *Charisma*. And she has impressive research, clinical evidence, years of experience, and common sense bolstering her claim. She is a well-known image consultant who conducts workshops and lectures at seminars on the subject of charisma and how to get it. Marcia has turned numerous shy, introverted, and unpopular adults into magnetic personalities. How this magic is accomplished is the main subject of this book.

Her message is dazzlingly clear: Charisma is neither an accident of genes, nor is it luck. The potential for charisma is our birthright — a natural gift given to each of us. But if this is the case, why do so few seem to possess it? Because most often it lies quietly dormant deep within the individual — held down, undeveloped, and hidden from view.

Until now, we have found it difficult to explain what charisma is and why some people seem to have it in abundance while the majority of others seem to have little or none at all. And we have been curious about how some people have charisma as children, then lose it, while others first get it later in life. And what about those who have it only at certain times — when at work, for example, but not in social situations, or, as is the case with many entertainers, when on stage but not when off?

This book first unravels these mysteries and then teaches us how to awaken the charismatic force within us, how to enhance its power, and how to sustain its magic. Development of our potential for charisma is a skill, we are told — a skill we can study, practice, master, and absorb as a part of ourselves. Anyone can do it and many individuals already have, simply by following Marcia Grad's highly effective, step-by-step Charisma Development Program.

What is this program that can help a shy person to become confident, an apathetic person to become enthusiastic, a dull person to become exciting, and everyone to have command of his or her own innate magnetism? The author uses a multidimensional approach. She explores the many pieces of the charisma puzzle, each essential to its solution — thoughts, attitudes, perceptions, social behavior, sexuality, physical presentation, and personal habits. We are urged to probe, to question, and to change longtime beliefs about ourselves, about others, and about the world that may be blocking the flow of our natural charisma. Then we are ready to start cultivating habits basic to building "that special magic." You will gain some surprising insights into how you behave in your daily life, and will be given specific techniques which will help to make charismatic feelings, behaviors, and qualities become second nature to you. Once mastered, these techniques work automatically, on a subconscious level. They become an integral part of your total being.

This book reflects the personal flair of its author whose enthusiasm and conviction that people can and do change have served as an inspiration to her many students and clients. The same expert guidance and continuous encouragement that have been invaluable to them are now available to you, the reader.

I'm especially pleased to endorse Marcia's book because I've seen the amazing results of her techniques. They work. Her students are now out in the world realizing their dreams. And what happened to them could happen to you.

You needn't become reconciled to remaining as you are. You can be as you've always wished to be — self-assured, in control in social and business situations, energetic, and stimulating to others. You can be noticed, be liked, and be sought after. You can meet the people you want to meet and bring them into your life. You can become involved in relationships you previously thought were beyond you, and you will be able to reach for business opportunities never before within your grasp.

If you've previously believed that only a select few individuals are capable of powerful personal magnetism and that, unluckily, you are not one of them, you are about to embark upon a unique and eye-opening journey. It's exhilarating just to imagine what is waiting for you — achievement of all those goals and aspirations you once thought impossible. This is your chance for a new beginning, for a new and better you, for a new and better life. I wish you success in achieving your goals.

Melvin Powers
Publisher, Wilshire Book Company

CONTENTS

PART ONE

THE SECRET OF CHARISMA

Chapter One

Emotional Rags to Riches

*Emotional wealth often grows out of
what appear to be poor experiences.*

This book is a product of my own emotional metamorphosis.
I think it is important for you to know me as I was and as I am
in order to understand this emotional rags-to-riches story that very
well may touch your own life.

I was the first baby of my generation born in the family. My
18-year-old father was sent to Europe to fight a war soon after
my birth, leaving his teen-age wife to manage on her own. Lonely
for her husband and estranged from her friends who were single
and actively participating in the war effort, she filled her days
with mothering and her nights with tears.

My mother wasn't the only one who was isolated from her con-
temporaries. I clearly remember endless hours of sitting on the
back steps of our second-story apartment watching longingly as
the children below played in the nursery school yard next door,
feeling left out, feeling different, and feeling undesirable. My
mother's pleas to allow me to play for just a few minutes a day
at recess time went unheard by the school's owner who said they
were already overcrowded.

A few years later, my father came home. He and I became acquainted and slowly adjusted to our respective roles of father and
daughter following a difficult period of "Do I have to do what
he says, Mommy?" He and my mother, virtually strangers, became
reacquainted.

When they knew my sister was on the way, we moved to a little
house in a suburb of Los Angeles. During the years I attended
elementary school there, I went home for lunch every day to a

loving mother, an appetizing meal, and the latest episode of "Crusader Rabbit" on *Sheriff John's Lunch Brigade*.

Mom was always there to share my triumphs and to soothe my hurts. My dad told me to give everything I attempted my best effort and I was thrilled by the sparkle in his eyes when he knew that I had. We were very much a family — with honeysuckle, fruit trees, and crisscrossed organdy curtains — and what we lacked in money, we made up for in love. I showed my two younger sisters how to do backward somersaults, how to spy on my parents' parties through the heating vent, and, generally, how to get along in the world.

But, of course, it wasn't all fairy tale perfect. There were times when my sisters and I engaged in squabbles — moments like you all probably had, times when we thought the thoughts of all children — that the rules were too strict, or that someone else was being favored above us. And there was the usual emotional insecurity that resulted from being raised in an era when parents made most of their children's decisions and transmitted to them firm messages as to what they should think and how they should feel and conduct their lives.

Because of my strong inclination to always be neat and clean, my peas never dared to roll into my mashed potatoes, and I could make mudpies while wearing a frilly dress without ever getting it dirty. And I was delicate. Playing dodgeball stung my legs; "Red Rover, Red Rover" made my arms ache. But I loved hopscotch — I couldn't get hurt or make a fool of myself playing hopscotch. I was a bit timid and very sensitive, and my burning desire was to be the beautiful singing and dancing lady in the old, romantic "boy-gets-girl" movies.

When I was 12 years old, I was confined to a polio ward in the Los Angeles County Hospital. I vividly remember the panic I felt when my parents talked to me through a microphone built into an all-glass viewing corridor that ran along the length of my room; when I felt the burning of the Sister Kenny steaming wool towels that I was repeatedly wrapped in; and when I realized that the masked, gloved nurses threw everything I touched into a contamination tank. I recall the odd sensation I felt when I tried to move my leg and it remained immobile, and, finally, the defeat I experienced when, ready to leave the hospital, I realized I couldn't walk. I even remember the look in people's eyes the first time I ventured into public in a wheelchair.

Then came the rehabilitation center and its gruelling physical-therapy classes, pinpointing weakness, producing frustration and the inevitable "Why me?" I remember the Olympic skier Jill Kinmont lying in the bed next to me, nearly totally paralyzed from a skiing accident that made headlines (and inspired the book and movie, *The Other Side of the Mountain),* smiling and encouraging me. I'll never forget her strength and how it helped to build mine.

There were many weekends spent at home, my wheelchair bumping into everything in our small house. Finally, I made the difficult transitions — first to crutches and then to the hospital handrails. I was limping, but making it on my own!

Still limping, I returned to school and, though somewhat of an oddity at first, I re-established friendships and managed to catch up in my classes. I had the usual teen-age dreams — to be chosen first at the Sports Night Dance, to be the first choice of Mr. Wonderful in front of entire student body, and to have a blond brush-up hair-do, full twirly petticoat, sling-back high-heeled shoes, and a carefree, confident manner so I could dance every dance with a different boy. However, for reasons I didn't understand, it was more likely that I would be chosen to dance with, to date, or to befriend only after the "best girls" were taken.

My family moved to a larger house — a real fixer-upper — in another part of Los Angeles. The friends I made at the high school in my new neighborhood were members of "Anora," a sorority whose members were those who "weren't right" for "Dantes" — the club chosen by the most popular girls. I felt as if my position always had been and would always be several rungs lower on the desirability ladder than those occupied by the poised, self-assured, "beautiful" people whom I found to be so intimidating. It seemed that I wasn't destined to be part of the "in" group. I decided to resign myself to being ordinary — and, oh, how hard I tried to accept that. I settled for "Anora" with its promise of emotional safety and social security.

While a high school senior, I met Jerry. After ten months, our developing friendship took on a new dimension — a growing love, a growing passion. We dated through three years of college, ceasing to see each other whenever we became too serious. We had to wait to marry; he was a pre-medical student.

Throughout my college years, my childhood dream of becoming an actress persisted though I regularly dismissed it as being totally impractical and ridiculously childish. I was an education major. (Teachers were very much in demand and the hours were convenient for a woman who planned to rear children.) But I couldn't resist the temptation to enroll in just one acting course. The thrill I felt when chosen to play a leading role was nothing compared to the ecstacy I experienced while performing it on stage. When I was in front of an audience, I became the someone who was all that I believed I could not be.

But who was I to think that I could "make it" in the theater when so many others had tried and most had failed? No. I wouldn't allow a seemingly impossible fantasy to divert me from the life course I was certain would practically guarantee my happiness — love and marriage.

After a date late one night in June, Jerry and I awakened my parents to tell them that we had planned a life together. We wanted to get married the following September, just two weeks before Jerry was to begin medical school. I would be student teaching (didn't almost all medical students marry teachers?) until my graduation in January. Then I would teach full-time while he finished school. We would pay back the tuition loans, have a family, and embark on a dream life of sustained happiness and fulfillment.

My parents loved Jerry as the son they didn't have. Our wedding was glorious; the honeymoon was even better. We were Mr. and Mrs. Madly-in-Love and were ready to take on the world.

We settled into a small, attractive apartment, filling it with hand-me-down furniture and wall-to-wall love. I was Suzy Homemaker, Mrs. Clean — and I adored every minute of it.

Many of Jerry's classmates seemed to be managing so well with new babies that we decided not to wait to begin our family.

My parents threw a big party to celebrate my twenty-first birthday, my college graduation, and the announcement of our first child due in August, just eleven months after our wedding. Everyone was so happy my dream was coming true. I was passionately in love with a wonderful man, was soon to have our baby, and was looking forward to a promised life of security and comfort — I had it all.

Most evenings I crocheted while Jerry studied at his big wooden desk right across from me in our living room. When we weren't at my parents' house for dinner, we survived on spaghetti, meatloaf, laughter, and dreams. We went to the movies on free passes or played cards with friends at potluck-dinners. We shared chores on Saturday mornings, and in the afternoon Jerry studied while I shopped, ran errands, and did lesson plans.

We moved to a two-bedroom apartment that we couldn't easily afford. August came, as did the labor pains one night while we had company. Everyone caravaned to the hospital for the big event.

Our son was born with a slight breathing problem. We were assured it would improve in a matter of hours, but his condition worsened and I was moved to a private room where Jerry stayed with me for two days and nights. Amid the gifts, balloons, and congratulatory flowers, frightened and in a state of disbelief, we reached out to each other for comfort. Then it was over — our baby died. The dream began to falter.

Jerry took two weeks off from his summer job selling plumbing and we went home, alone, to our apartment from which my heartbroken mother had removed all the baby things. We loved and consoled each other, and I cried until my tears ran dry.

My doctors recommended that I become pregnant again as soon as possible. We followed their advice — I was once again expecting in August.

Jerry returned to school, and I went to work at an electric company. The pay was less than I could have made teaching, but I couldn't bear to work with small children again. Because we had been unable to afford medical insurance, the considerable bills we incurred trying to save our baby had to be paid off little by little.

While still struggling to deal with the death of our first baby, I discovered I had a new problem. My tower of strength — my husband — began to feel the full impact of the previous year. He was tired of school, of student loans, of medical bill payments, and of my having to work. He quit medical school to accept a "real job." The dream disintegrated further.

Our daughter, Laura, was born healthy. And the joy we shared helped to heal the old wound.

Jerry worked hard and long at a succession of several jobs trying to make enough money to pay off our debts. Our life was difficult in some respects, but we had the child we'd prayed for, a house with a lovely yard where she could play, many fun-filled times together, and our love for one another. And that was enough — or was it?

There were years of day-to-day coping with an illness I had that became evident right after the birth of our third child, a son named Robert. There were lengthy hospital stays, a severely restricted diet, daily injections, and dependency on several potent drugs.

In addition, there were the usual family catastrophies, big and small: our daughter's bout with dislocated cervical discs requiring traction and a panicked race to a hospital oxygen tent when once she suddenly stopped breathing; Jerry's chronic kidney stone attacks requiring four hospital stays and one emergency appendectomy; three or four (who can remember?) surgeries for me and one miscarriage; one earthquake evacuation from our damaged home; and one near-entrapment in a hotel fire.

We had a couple of tranquil years when we were all reasonably healthy. Jerry was managing a chain of retail stores, so we were doing better financially, too. If at times I felt a little empty and living seemed to require more effort than I had to give — well, possibly those feelings were to be expected. Years of illness and semi-confinement to my house had left me physically depleted, emotionally depressed, and more unsure of myself socially than ever before.

I tried to ease myself back into the outside world by doing volunteer work at a local hospital two mornings a week. As I became more comfortable being with people, I began to teach children again, part time. My self-confidence increased just enough for me to make several unsuccessful attempts to start my own business, and I wondered whether anything in my life would ever again run smoothly. During this time, I tried to get into better physical condition. I attended a semi-weekly yoga class, learned to play tennis, and ran regularly at the local college track.

But my progress was halted abruptly when my car was hit by a truck. One ambulance ride and one hospital visit, and my days were once more filled with physical-therapy treatments and constant pain.

After nine months, as the pain began to let up and I was piecing my restricted life back together, there was another automobile accident. Again, there was the hospital, the physical-therapy treatments, the unceasing pain, and, this time, emotional exhaustion. My personal life was well disintegrated and my marital relationship was right behind.

Jerry's and my love for each other became buried under the

weight of new problems. The dream finally blew apart. We separated.

After a period of adjustment, I settled down to a single life with my children. Feeling emotionally low, I hesitatingly ventured out into the modern singles scene. Once again, as in my youth, I found myself frustrated by and envious of those lucky, specially endowed individuals who seemed to be able to attract whomever they desired. I quickly grew tired of trying to appear as an active participant at parties by making frequent trips to food tables and restrooms. When I approached a man whom I wanted to meet, he inevitably turned his attention to the woman standing next to me. When, occasionally, I managed to meet someone new and interesting, I often was too nervous to even look directly at him, much less to think of anything to say.

It seems that sometimes we have to hit rock bottom before facing a problem and making a decision to not retreat from the world but, rather, to learn to function more effectively within it. Soon after reaching that point, with the help of a dear, sensitive confidante and an outstanding marriage counselor guiding me, the realization of what I had been — an expert sufferer — slowly pervaded my mind. Life had treated me roughly and I had made myself emotionally distraught and sometimes physically sick by fighting what I perceived as its unfairness and its cruelty. No one had come to my rescue nor bailed me out of my various miseries. I finally faced the fact that no one ever would nor could. I would have to do it myself.

I began to redigest portions of self-help books that I had read, and I avidly devoured many new ones. I remembered stories that people had related to me about their own lives and feelings, searching for subtle messages I may previously have missed. I went through the tumultuous experience of systematically examining myself and my life. I thought about Jill Kinmont at the rehabilitation center and her incredible enthusiasm for living, her warmth, and her smile.

It didn't take long before I realized that I needed to make some big changes in my basic, lifelong attitudes about myself, about the way I perceived life, and about my relationships with other people. I longed to feel happy and I worked very hard to learn how. I found out that happiness isn't something to demand, to chase after, or to be given. It will come from inside each of us when we know what to look for, how to find it, and how to share it.

Slowly, I emerged from my metamorphosis filled with happiness — the kind that makes you smile when no one is looking and hum when you're all alone — and an inner peace and contentment such as I had never known. I developed an enthusiasm for greeting life as it came — good or bad, easy or hard. I drew strength from each of my past difficulties until my inner core became solid and reliable. I knew I would always be there for me; I could count on me. I learned to accept myself just as I was, to like myself, to enjoy myself, and even to get a kick out of myself now and then. I had finally become free to fully experience and to appreciate the various facets of myself and of the world around me. And I became able to confidently and joyfully share my real self and my excitement for living with other people.

When I began doing so, something unexpected happened. People began to notice me and to seek me out. My new approach to life not only made me feel wonderful, it obviously made other people feel good, too. I thrived on the positive responses I was getting from others. I knew that my power to attract people was increasing.

I carefully observed those whom I considered to have powerful personal magnetism. I noticed every aspect of their appearances and social behaviors. And I talked with many of them to find out more about their ability to attract people.

Although I had previously doubted it, I began to believe that perhaps charisma *could* be developed. Tired of being one of those individuals who didn't "have it," I became determined to find out whether or not I could learn to be one of those who did "have it."

I excitedly escalated my self-improvement program. I combined and recombined various psychological philosophies, expanding on some and discarding others. I experimented with new ways of thinking, diligently practiced new behaviors, and worked to enhance my appearance. My ability to attract others and to sustain their interest continued to increase. I had discovered the secret of creating charisma — the magic I had yearned to possess.

No longer did I have to be concerned about how and where to meet new people. I began to meet them everywhere — at the auto-repair shop, in my dentist's waiting room, and at the supermarket. I easily made friends with classmates and instructors of seminars that I attended. My social calendar was full. At parties,

I frequently was the center of attraction — just like the popular girls I had so often watched and envied from the sidelines.

Relationships with my parents and sisters became enriched as I exhibited a new depth of caring and sharing. They were amazed by the drastic change in me, as were longtime friends who found it difficult to believe that I was the same unhappy, inhibited lady whom they had known for so many years. Laura and Robbie began to call me their "new mom." Eventually, the old fire of my marital relationship was rekindled. Jerry came home.

Business and professional opportunities abounded as did social ones. Enthusiastic potential partners and offers of challenging positions emerged when I least expected them to. I had exciting choices to consider that never before had existed. I tried a variety of endeavors, many of which proved to be satisfyingly successful, such as the publication of my first book and the establishment of my own public-relations firm. My newly found energetic, positive attitude elicited corresponding responses from people. It made my ventures much more likely to prosper than before. Almost anything seemed possible — even the realization of unlikely dreams.

However, becoming the "new me" brought no guarantee that I would enjoy an untroubled life. More turbulent years followed during which my family struggled with everything that makes movies top box-office hits. There was a succession beyond belief of soap-opera style, real-life problems and crises — various members' distressing, new physical conditions, disturbing emotional ones, and an assortment of personal traumas, including a painful divorce.

So do I still manage to smile when no one is looking and to hum when I'm all alone? I certainly do. And so can you.

I've shared my personal story with you to prove it is untrue that "people can't change." You *can* transform yourself into the person you may always have wished to become. No matter how difficult your life may have been or may now be, no matter how much you need to improve to elicit the response you want from others — *you can do it.* You have the power to change yourself, your life, and your impact on people.

I am writing this book to show you how and, I hope, to inspire you to develop your own charisma. Awakening the charismatic power within you may be the most important experience you'll ever have, promising more rewards to you for your efforts than for anything else you've ever undertaken. Give yourself this opportunity for a new and better life.

Chapter Two

What Is Charisma?
The Secret Revealed

*Unravel the mystery of charisma and you
will discover the true essence of life.*

Undoubtedly, you have seen them — those special individuals whose mere presence can electrify an entire roomful of people. They exude confidence that commands attention. Others gravitate toward them, seemingly entranced by every word they say. Perhaps you have become fascinated by such a person and find it difficult to identify what causes this individual to have a magical effect on you. Maybe you believe this person was born with an ability to attract as one is born with blue eyes or a large bone structure. We know this is not true. Eleanor Roosevelt's tremendous appeal to the public did not surface until she became an adult. Conversely, some people "have it" as children but seem to "lose it" on their way to adulthood.

MASTERS OF PERSONAL MAGNETISM

Political personages and spiritual leaders are masters of this magic — the names of John F. Kennedy, Robert Kennedy, Evita Peron, Jacqueline Kennedy Onassis and Mahatma Gandhi come to mind, as do movie stars Elizabeth Taylor and Robert Redford and musical entertainers Neil Diamond, Frank Sinatra, Elvis Presley, and Michael Jackson. Phil Donahue, Johnny Carson, and Merv Griffin keep audiences glued to their television sets, logging hundreds of hours, year after year. They all have held people spellbound with their magnetism.

What is this magnetic force that enables some people to capture and to hold the spotlight? It's charisma — that "mysterious something" that we can instantly identify in some people.

Charisma was originally defined by the Greeks as favor or divine gift, such as the power to heal or to prophesy. It was redefined in this century by the German economist and sociologist Max Weber, who wrote that charisma is "a certain quality of an individual personality by virtue of which he is set apart from ordinary men and treated as endowed with supernatural, superhuman, or at least specifically exceptional powers or qualities." In his voluminous writings on the subject, he broadened the concept of charisma to include creative or innovative personalities who gather followings, although they do not claim to possess divine grace. Today, the term charisma has a more general meaning because of its liberal use by sociologists, social scientists, and psychologists. Its many labels include personal magnetism, charm, star quality, and winning personality.

Charisma is a multifaceted phenomenon. In public figures it takes many forms, each dependent upon somewhat different components. We have loved political leaders who offered us hope in times of great social need, as did Franklin Delano Roosevelt during the Depression. We have been moved by and have witnessed vast societal changes occurring as a result of the passionate convictions and unrelenting efforts of charismatic people committed to a cause, as was Martin Luther King, Jr. And we have seen the wholehearted devotion, blind fanatical trust, and unconditional faith given such destructive leaders as Adolf Hitler, Charles Manson, and the Reverend Jim Jones.

Often the charismatic power of political leaders is partially dependent upon factors outside themselves. Roosevelt, Mussolini, and Hitler all came to power after periods of war, inflation, and/or depression. People's dissatisfaction with the way things were and their readiness for social change made them susceptible to the persuasions of leaders who they believed had "the answer." Some such individuals who offered encouragement and new direction were elevated by their followers to god-like stature.

Spiritual leaders, to an extent, are dependent upon the needs of their followers in order to be perceived as charismatic. Those individuals who effectively use their ability to feed the human spirit are capable of creating an aura that has strong influence upon their followers. Billy Graham, one of the most popular evangelists of all time, has redirected the lives of millions. Pope John Paul II inspires immense crowds by sharing intimate moments and by persuading them that they are capable of higher deeds, of more love, and of greater compassion than they ever thought possible.

Superstars fulfill needs other than those met by political and spiritual leaders, such as the desire for stimulation, for enjoyment, for diversion, and for beauty.

While it is true that our own psychic requirements create an environment in which a charismatic leader or star can flourish, certain qualities of personality are necessary to project a magnetic image. Were this not true, we would find that everyone who professes to have a mission, a calling, a solution that would benefit us, or who appears to be able to fulfill us in some way would be charismatic.

Although not all charismatic leaders possess exactly the same combination of qualities, there appear to be some that are commonly held. Though numerous people have one or more of these attributes, charismatic individuals tend to possess them in extraordinary amounts — high-energy level, sustained vitality, courage, composure (especially when under stress), strong sense of self, clear direction and movement toward one's goal or goals, and determination to succeed.

The paradox is that while we like to look up to, respect, admire, and perhaps be in awe of charismatic individuals, we are most strongly attracted to them when we can, at the same time, relate to and identify with them as human beings. We want to feel that they are, in some way, ordinary people just like us.

Because recognizing someone as charismatic is an emotional reaction rather than an intellectual decision, we respond intensely to individuals who touch our innermost emotional selves. For this reason, many qualities which may be viewed as being negative can actually enhance a person's charisma.

We sympathize with individuals who have subtle flaws, and our compassion is aroused by those who have obvious defects. Vulnerabilities help us to feel the realness of those who otherwise might seem to be remote or too perfect. And personal struggles to overcome emotional and physical handicaps and adversities can add greatly to their charisma, as can a dramatic brush with death.

FDR's wheelchair, JFK's back problems, Winston Churchill's lisp, Marilyn Monroe's spicy fragility, and Jimmy Durante's tremendous nose all served as charisma-boosting aids.

A variety of other characteristics can also increase the likelihood of a person projecting charisma. An accent or other foreignism — almost anything that is exotic or mysterious — intrigues us. And an aura of power, vast wealth, or fame can fuel one's perception of charisma as can unusual talent, exceptional intellect, or great beauty. We are impressed by those who possess these attributes and the stronger and more developed they become, the greater is the attractiveness of the individual.

Can you ever hope to possess strong personal magnetism without the help of such attributes? Yes, because, fortunately, one's ability to be charismatic is not solely dependent upon one's promises, social position, talents, IQ, or accomplishments. You can develop powerful charisma without the aid of qualities that appear to be superhuman or that are imposing or awe-inspiring. Charisma can be generated by developing the potential that is within each of us. Knowingly or unknowingly, you probably have already experienced your own charisma. Recognizing it in its various forms is the first step to harnessing its power.

THREE TYPES OF CHARISMA

Pseudo-Charisma

Actors, politicians, professional speakers, auctioneers, salespeople, and others whose success depends upon winning us over learn to "turn on the charm" when it is needed. Often they acquire the ability to make us trust them and to believe in them. These individuals know that the way they look, talk, move, and even think determine the strength of their impact on us. They use charisma as a tool to help them accomplish specific desired ends.

Pseudo-Charisma is also used by people in everyday situations to impress the boss, to attract a date, or to get others to follow their wishes. Sometimes we can sense that such a person's "charisma" is nothing more than a carefully constructed image of themselves. This illusion can be effective — at least temporarily.

Real Situational Charisma

Sometimes people spontaneously become turned on by what they are doing or by something that is happening at the moment. When this occurs to an individual who is performing on stage, for example, he or she goes with the flow and gets caught up in the excitement of a natural high. But such a person is not always able to generate this stimulating energy in other situations.

One television show host commented that he finds it easy to charm his nationwide audience, but that he is a "basket case at a cocktail party." Many people in the entertainment industry are confident when onstage but are shy when offstage. In the same way, a business person can be commanding at meetings but be timid when on a date. Or, one can be dull when at work but become stimulating when excitedly talking about a pet topic or when participating in a favorite pastime.

Real Situational Charisma is the result of feeling exceptionally good about oneself in a particular situation. We experience it when we feel accepted and appreciated, as when we are in love, are promoted, or do something of which we are especially proud. At these times, our self-esteem is increased, and it affects how we are perceived by others.

Have you ever seen a friend who had just fallen madly in love and been immediately aware that she was experiencing something wonderful and uplifting? Perhaps you wondered why this person looked so radiant and whether she had just returned from a dream vacation or had won a big sweepstakes. Didn't she have a spring in her walk and seem to stand taller, appear more outgoing and self-assured than before? Wasn't her voice lively and the sparkle in her eyes exciting?

Individuals who possess Real Situational Charisma spontaneously and energetically release their good feelings in some situations, but are unable to reproduce and share them at will.

Genuine Sustained Charisma

People who possess Genuine Sustained Charisma are able to maintain an excitement about themselves that lasts far beyond their initial, momentary, favorable impact on others and beyond the stimulation of temporary situations. Their charisma seems to be an intrinsic part of who they are. These individuals know how to produce and reproduce charisma. They have mastered the magic — and so can you.

At one time or another, we have all experienced moments of feeling at one with ourselves and the world. We have been aware of a positive glow about ourselves that for a minute, an hour, or a day colored our thoughts and enhanced how we felt and behaved. At those times, we attracted others more readily than usual.

How charismatic we are depends partly upon the length of time we experience these good feelings, their degree of intensity, and how free we are to share them with others.

BEING MAGNETIC IS OUR NATURAL STATE

We are dull and boring only when we are too inhibited or too afraid to share our real selves with others. We erect psychological barriers which block the flow of our natural charisma — that distinctive part of our personality that others might find to be the most fascinating. Charisma is felt deep within us. It can help us to attract people when we learn how to develop it and set it free.

Why do so many of us have difficulty releasing our charisma? Unfortunately, as we grow up we often are taught to contain and hide it from others. We are conditioned when we are told, "don't touch," "act grown up," and admonished to keep our emotions in check. We further imprison our natural potential for charisma by building elaborate defense networks to protect us from life's little discomforts.

We react instinctively to people who dare to be open with us and who are fun-loving and spontaneous without fear of judgment or rejection, and who self-confidently communicate a sincere, appreciative, enthusiastic interest in others and in the world around them. We seek out these people. They brighten our lives, help relieve our bouts of boredom caused by the tedious aspects of living, and momentarily make us forget our day-to-day concerns. Their inner glow and their special sparkle make them different, refreshing, and stimulating. Such people are emotionally rich. The sharing of their abundant, unique inner vitality is the sunshine that lights up a room when they enter.

Aren't we immediately aware of the positive vibrations emanating from such an individual? It could be a salesperson, a potential business associate, friend, or lover — anyone. We meet, and instantly we know whether we like or dislike this person. If we like him or her, chances are we are responding to the subtle mystique of power the likeable, attractive personality effortlessly exudes. When we dislike the person, we are receiving negative vibrations — charisma working in reverse. Our intuitive sixth sense is deeply involved in our seemingly automatic, subliminal reaction to people, but it is not the only sense which relays an impression to us.

THE PHENOMENON OF A CHARISMATIC FIRST IMPRESSION

When meeting someone new, we notice first how that person looks. We are instantly aware of his or her gender, age, and skin color. Then we focus on other physical attributes, such as height, weight, body configuration, hair, and the many other components, such as clothing, which contribute to his or her physical appearance.

We see and react to a person's facial expressions and body language, including eye contact, posture, gestures, use of personal space, and touch. These elements comprise 55 percent of one's first impression of others.

Next, we focus on what we hear. A person's vocal quality, force, pitch, articulation, and level of emotion comprise another 38 percent of our judgment of people.

Conversation — the actual words an individual speaks — makes up the final 7 percent of a person's total initial impact.

Components of a First Impression

55% NONVERBAL COMMUNICATION	38% VOCAL COMPONENT	7% VERBAL COMPONENT
Facial expression Body language	Way in which words are spoken	Actual words and their meanings

Our attitude and the way we look, talk, and move determine how others perceive us. If we fall short in any area, especially during the first few crucial minutes after meeting someone, we risk "turning off" others. And once we create a negative first impression, it is difficult, if not impossible, to change it.

Have you ever thought someone new sounded wonderful on the telephone but felt your excitement wane when seeing this person for the first time? Perhaps ill manners, poor grooming, irritating nervous habits, or some other negative quality or behavior disappointed you and destroyed your previous interest in this individual. Or maybe upon meeting an attractive and impeccably dressed person, you became disenchanted when you encountered his or her self-conscious or abrasive manner, or monotonous or whining voice.

In a sense, we market ourselves as one markets any product. For instance, a new book may be a literary masterpiece but if its title and cover are unappealing, few people may ever know the beauty of what's inside. Conversely, we may be enticed to read a book by its dazzling cover and stimulating title, but for it to hold our interest, it must say something interesting or different.

Our appearance, too, serves to draw people's attention to us, giving them an opportunity to discover our internal desirable qualities — qualities that enhance our appearance, for our walk, posture, facial expressions, voice, and conversation all reflect our emotional state. Our minds and bodies are inexplicably interrelated.

Charismatic individuals know that their power to attract people is dependent upon their skill to project their best possible inner and outer selves. When they do so, they are able to captivate others as if by magic.

We, too, can become spellbinders by fueling the usual elements required to make a good first impression with our fiery inner energy and enthusiasm. Utilization of inter-personal know-how and natural vitality can elevate a good impression to one that is powerfully charismatic.

INSTANT CHARISMA — WHAT IS THE MAGIC?

What is the mystique that enchants people? It's as unexplainable as is the phenomenon of, at times, feeling the presence of someone watching us from behind. It's as undefinable as romance and the human spirit, yet you can learn how to spark its power.

Research psychologists have found that when we experience an immediate, intense attraction to someone, our excitement causes our bodies to go through a chain of chemical reactions that makes our hearts and breathing speed up. We feel nervously excited and full of anticipation. The chemicals that cause these reactions continue to circulate in our bodies, stimulating our nervous systems even further and intensifying and perpetuating our original excitement. We can learn how to trigger in others this bodily chemical reaction that can transform their momentary interest in us to fascination with us.

Strong, pleasurable stimulation of our senses can create the original excitement that causes this entire physiological process to begin. It is possible that we may be able to create the magic of immediate charismatic attraction by evolving to a point where we are flooding people's senses with electrifying, pleasure-producing signals.

Charisma is a magnetic attraction created by a delicate balance of these potent signals broadcast by one person and received subconsciously by another. Although we can attract on different levels — intellectual, emotional, or physical — these signals are most effective when they are the result of one's total essence — how one stands and moves, grooms and dresses, expresses oneself, thinks, believes, feels, and behaves.

We can readily see some of these signals. Others are less apparent. Although once considered mysterious, invisible energy waves, positive and negative electrical charges, and electro-magnetic phenomena are now scientifically accepted as part of the life process. The electrical currents conducted by brain and muscle activity have been measured by electronic recording devices. Rapidly fluctuating positive and negative electrical charges have been verified and well documented as existing at the cellular level. And a special method called Kirlian photography has made visible an ordinarily imperceptible electro-magnetic field which surrounds every living thing. Pictures of these fields, or auras as they are often referred to, taken by numerous researchers around the world show some to be barely visible while others are larger and brilliantly colored. Variations in intensity and frequency have been found not only between people, but within the same person at different times. It is believed that the energy inherent in the precious, unduplicable life force gives off charges that creates a person's aura. When we develop and release our inner energy, we may increase the strength of these electrical signals, perhaps explaining the "vibes" we frequently refer and react to subconsciously.

Whatever the exact nature of charismatic attraction, an individual who develops and refines the ability to broadcast *all* the various types of positive signals maximizes his or her potential for charismatic power.

ANYONE CAN DEVELOP CHARISMA

At its best, charisma is a blend of specific attitudinal, behavioral, personal, physical, and social skills. As with all skills, it can be improved with practice. We can train ourselves to be charismatic as surely as we can learn to type, to dance, or to play tennis or the piano. While certain people may find it easier than others to master these skills, with perseverance anyone can greatly improve

his or her ability to attract people and to win their continuing
interest and esteem.

Chapter Three

How to Awaken the Charismatic Power Within You: The Charisma Development Program

*Charisma is our birthright. One needs
only to learn how to claim it.*

HOW THE CHARISMA DEVELOPMENT PROGRAM FIRST BEGAN

Originally, I developed the program in an effort to increase my own power to attract people. I carefully chose, adapted, and conscientiously used the best of all the psychological tools available to me — dozens of self-help books and the exceedingly useful self-esteem-raising and behavior-modifying techniques I gleaned from seminars and psychological consultations. And I created and extensively practiced exercises designed specifically to achieve and then maintain that much-sought-after charismatic aura.

HOW THE PROGRAM WAS TESTED AND PROVED EFFECTIVE

As a publicist, I shared these techniques with numerous authors over a period of more than five years, as I worked with them to build their charismatic qualities. Many of their lives began to flourish as they learned how to employ effective ways of thinking and behaving, how to make the most of their physical assets and the least of their liabilities, and how to diligently practice a variety of personal, physical, and social skills. Those who persevered developed appealing personalities that helped them attract new friends, establish new romances, enliven existing relationships, enrich their work, increase their productivity, and add immeasurably to their general happiness and well-being. At present, I teach students at colleges throughout the Los Angeles area how to develop charisma. I conduct charisma workshops and lecture to groups and to the business community, using the same techniques that proved so effective for my author-clients.

Just three months after attending the charisma class, petite, 32-year-old Karen, whom I remembered as being nice but rather ordinary, bounced into my office, her soft, brown eyes twinkling. "I just had to come and tell you what's happening to me. Ever since I can remember, I've wanted desperately to feel special and to be noticed right away by others. Well, my dream is finally coming true. Last night I went to a party knowing hardly anyone, and I left knowing almost everyone. People just kept coming around to talk and to dance. I was the real me and everybody loved it. What a great feeling! Not only that — everything seems to be going right. I enjoy everyday things more, you know, like talking to other customers in the market or visiting with the counter girl at the dry cleaners. Even greeting people at my teller's window in the bank is now fun. I seem to see everything through new, happy eyes."

The Charisma Development Program that helped Karen has been used successfully with entertainers, politicians, business and professional people and with those who have special image needs.

YOU ARE A RESERVOIR OF UNTAPPED POTENTIAL

Although Karen once considered herself to be incapable of projecting charisma, she found that she was a reservoir of untapped potential — and so are you. The thrilling prospect is that no one can predict what that potential really is. It's limitless. When you unlock your charismatic power and put it to work for you, every goal that you put your mind to becomes attainable.

Why not live every day of your life to the fullest? Why not have more fulfilling friendships, the love relationships you may have longed for, and success in your business life? You can discard old limitations and know the ecstacy of achieving your most cherished aspirations.

Do you want to become more attractive and exciting than you

are now? Perhaps you want to learn the secrets of developing a fascinating personality that will help you to get more of the good things in life — appreciation, love, recognition, and rewards. Regardless of your original motivation for wanting to be charismatic, its subtle influence will permeate and enrich every facet of your life.

TRANSFORM YOURSELF INTO THE PERSON YOU MAY HAVE SECRETLY YEARNED TO BECOME

Perhaps you've read that anyone can develop a winning personality and be attractive, charming, and exciting; yet, somehow, you doubt your ability to project these characteristics. Maybe you've tried to be more popular or to change your appearance or parts of your personality in an effort to improve your impact on others, but you've failed to see any results. Now you can transform yourself into the person you may have secretly yearned to become by following a new, highly effective, step-by-step program designed to increase your power to attract people.

If you dream of being popular and accepted as one of the "in" group and want to be noticed, liked, and sought-after by others, or if you want to have influence, power, or authority in your personal or business life, here is your opportunity to make those dreams become realities. Whether you wish to project a subtle, compelling charm or to be captivating in a more dynamic way, be encouraged. People can and do become charismatic individuals. Numerous men and women, young and old, married and single, well-known and unknown have successfully achieved their goals and realized their dreams — and so can you.

WHAT IS THE CHARISMA DEVELOPMENT PROGRAM?

The objective of the program is to help each individual develop his or her own charismatic potential. It accommodates differing charismatic styles since what may be an instinctive manifestation of one person's charisma may be artificial and ineffective for someone else. And it is flexible so as to suit people's varying needs and existing developmental levels. The program has been designed to help one acquire and improve each of the elements of genuine sustained charisma.

Elements of Genuine Sustained Charisma

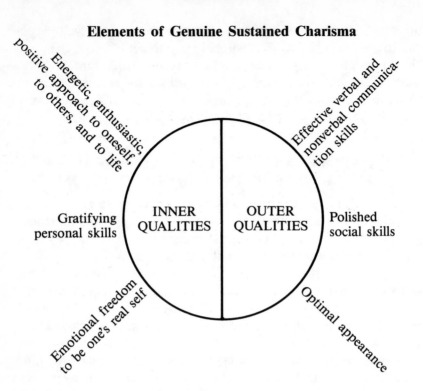

Charisma is the "polished realness" derived from these elements working together. It is the end result of projecting our best physical, emotional, spiritual, and behavioral selves.

The program is divided into two parts. Part one concentrates on development of the inner person and includes two stages. The first stage involves identifying and freeing oneself from the attitudes which cause a person to hold back his or her natural charisma. The second stage emphasizes enlivening one's personality and creating and sustaining a charismatic aura.

Part two of the program concerns development of the outer person, including techniques for improving verbal and nonverbal communication and social skills and methods of improving one's appearance.

It's exhilarating just to imagine what this program can mean to you. So, if you have decided to join those who are reaping the great benefits of their own quest for self-growth, get set for a thrilling adventure!

PART TWO

BRIGHTENING UP THE INNER YOU

Chapter Four

Identifying Your
Charisma-Blocking Beliefs

*Your personality is the outward
expression of your inner self.*

Arlene Francis once wrote that it doesn't pay to put good
wallpaper over crumbly plaster. Similarly, it is necessary to properly prepare the foundation upon which one's attractiveness rests.
It is ineffective to apply superficial finishing touches to one's personality before first getting rid of the fundamental negative beliefs
which block one's natural charisma. They are part of a well-
developed belief system that we all have underlying our emotions
and behaviors.

Where do these beliefs originate? Early in life we trusted and
accepted what others said about us and the world. We hold onto
these childish impressions though they may be grossly erroneous
at the time we form them or may become inaccurate as changes
occur through the years. Regardless, we reinforce them by believing that they *are* accurate and by acting accordingly. By so doing,
we make them become self-fulfilling prophecies. Subconsciously,
we literally make ourselves become what we believe ourselves to
be, and we make happen what we expect to transpire. For example, individuals who feel inadequate may avoid situations in which
they might experience success. Unsure of themselves, they hesitatingly attempt new undertakings while fearfully holding back their
best efforts, insuring that they will not do well. Their poor perfor-
mances reinforce their original belief that they could not do well.
This cycle of negative reinforcement perpetuates itself, often dooming such people to lives of varying degrees of self-consciousness,
timidity, insecurity, general dissatisfaction, and/or unhappiness.

Although these old, prepackaged, unquestioned beliefs, attitudes, and philosophies are capable of poisoning our lives and contaminating our spirits, most often we allow them to continue unchallenged and to restrain us from becoming all that we are capable of being. Some of these beliefs cause us to radiate powerful negative energy that repels others and produces a panorama of stresses, strains, and tensions.

Your ability to attract people depends upon your becoming aware of what your beliefs are and how you are being affected by them.

The groundwork for my own attitudinal and behavioral changes was laid when I began to list many of my basic beliefs. Years later, while I was working with authors, it became apparent to me that many people hold the same toxic beliefs. As a result, I compiled a list of those which I found to be the most widely held. I divided it into three categories — self-valuations, unrealistic expectations, and delusions.

Carefully think through each of the following charisma-blocking beliefs and decide whether or not it is part of your own belief system. If you agree with the belief as stated, think it is true for you, is like you, or affects your behavior, place a check on the line provided. If, however, you do not accept the belief, it is unlike you, and you do not hold it responsible for your perspective or behavior, leave it blank. Some of the beliefs are simply desires or opinions that many of us have but which become problematic only when exaggerated into absolutist "ought tos," "have tos," "musts," and "shoulds." So consider the degree of intensity of each when deciding which ones apply to you.

CHARISMA-BLOCKING BELIEFS

Self-Valuations

_____ 1. I *must* (not *just like to*) be approved of, accepted, and/or loved by almost everyone.

Whenever others think well of you, you're up and feel great; but when they think poorly of you, you're down and feel badly. Good feelings about yourself are dependent upon other people feeling good about you.

You may go to great lengths to get approval and to avoid disapproval by pretending or trying to be as others want you to be, by filling various roles and living up to stereotypes as others conceive of them, and by putting everyone else's needs and desires before your own. Your appetite for love and acceptance may sometimes seem to be insatiable.

You continuously rate yourself using other people's opinions of you as a measuring stick.

_____ 2. I *have* (not *just want*) to do well at everything. I *should* always be right and not make mistakes.

When you do well at any task, you feel good about yourself; but when you do poorly, fail at anything, or make a mistake, you feel downgraded.

You may procrastinate, have difficulty making decisions, and be hesitant to try new things because you don't want to risk being wrong or seeming incapable or foolish.

You continuously rate yourself using your performance level as a measuring stick.

_____ 3. I judge myself by others' standards and by comparing myself to other people.

I judge others by my standards and by comparing them to me.

I *should* be different from what I am.

Whenever you hold your own in comparison with others or meet their standards, you feel adequate, okay, and acceptable. When you surpass them or their standards, you feel superior — on top of the world. But when they or their standards surpass you, you feel inferior, second-rate, and miserable.

You may spend much time playing catch-up and perfecting your one-upmanship, forever striving to be good, better, best. You may be intimidated by others who have more money, status, power, fame, beauty, or intelligence than you. And you may feel an urgent need to have the material things that some others have, or feel compelled to go along with whatever is in fashion — whether it be a designer brand or a particular style of clothing, a certain make of automobile, a type of home furnishing, or a popular vacation spot — just because it is "in," barely considering whether you will really derive pleasure from it. You need to be part of the group.

You may think that you should be smarter, more artistic or scientific, more vivacious or reserved than you are, even though it might be inconsistent with your nature.

You continuously rate yourself using set standards and other persons as measuring sticks.

Throwing Away the Measuring Stick

Self-valuations are based on the assumption that you must earn and/or prove your self-worth repeatedly. You are vulnerable not because you are actually inferior, but because you keep comparing and evaluating yourself, depreciating your worth when you think that you don't measure up. Others' opinions, how well you do at various tasks, and how you stack up against others or your own childhood standards dictate whether you accept and like, or reject and dislike, yourself at any given moment. As long as your self-esteem is riding on these outside influences, you will be stuck on an emotional roller coaster that will greatly affect your morale and your impact on others.

You can step off this turbulent ride when you:

Accept that you are intrinsically good just as you are: perfect though fallible, possessing both strengths and weaknesses which is as it should be.

Know that although you may wish to improve, you don't have to be more, better, or different from what you are. You are simply you, and that is exactly who you are supposed to be.

Rely on your own judgment, preferring to follow your own direction rather than that of someone else and to risk making your own mistakes.

Count on yourself to come through for you (even if sometimes it is a struggle), knowing that you can and will successfully help yourself through anything, no matter how difficult the problem.

Take notice of, appreciate, and learn to admire the good qualities in the inner you — the deep part that makes you who you are.

Then, no one else's opinion of you nor any momentary failure to do well will shake your faith or belief in yourself as a good, valuable, dependable, lovable person.

Unrealistic Expectations

_____ 4. Others *should* think, feel, and do things as I want them to.

Frequently, you find yourself judging people's opinions and actions, and feel compelled to police them and to set them right. If they are resistant to your attempts to convince, convert, or manipulate them into your way of thinking, you might become frustrated or angry.

Why is this expectation unrealistic?

It's unrealistic because people will act in their own self-interest, consistent with their unique natures, regardless of what you say or do. Their perceptions, reactions, preferences, and desires are based on beliefs and attitudes created by their own knowledge and experiences. And they usually know what is best for them better than you do. If you try hard to get them to think or do as you want, they will probably be resentful and hostile, no matter who "wins." Either way, no one really benefits.

Just as your standards and goals may not work well for others, theirs may not be suitable for you. You needn't live up to anyone's expectations nor let them decide what will make you happy. Only you can decide what is best for you. You are the one who ultimately reaps the rewards or suffers the consequences of your own choices. Everyone must seek happiness in a manner consistent with his or her own nature.

_____ 5. I *should* be treated as I want to be treated.

You think it is only right for others to give you that which you perceive as your just due and to treat you in accordance with what you believe you deserve — to appreciate, to trust, or to respect you. Or, you may think they owe you help, support, consideration, attention, or love.

When you do not get from others that to which you think you are entitled, you may feel hurt, slighted, or used. Often you may think that you are giving more to others than you are getting from them. You may grumble and complain or become angry and quarrelsome.

Why is this expectation unrealistic?

Because although you may think that you deserve to be treated well, others see you through their own eyes, clouded by their own prejudices, preferences, and previous perceptions. They react to you in keeping with their own attitudes and beliefs, standards and desires.

When you expect others to treat you in any particular way, you're setting yourself up to be frequently disappointed. Often, the less you expect, the better for everyone. When you anticipate little and receive a lot, you'll be surprised and delighted; when you are treated poorly, you'll be able to calmly examine the situation and take steps to improve it rather than making it worse by starting an argument or storing up resentments.

_____ 6. I *should* get what I want out of life.

You think that you have the right to get from life whatever you desire, whether it be joy and fulfillment, good health, or material success. When life does not provide you with these, you may feel disillusioned and blame life for being unjust or too difficult. You may think that other people get all the breaks.

And you believe that life should not impose upon you anything that you don't want — financial problems, poor health, or loneliness, for example. When things don't go your way, you tend to damn fate and curse your rotten luck, or you may feel that it's unfair for your life to be burdensome when some others have it so easy.

Why is this expectation unrealistic?

You weren't born into this life with promises of fairness and justice. Life guarantees you nothing and owes you nothing. There is no one to set your life right but you. If you think some things would be better if changed, you can work to bring it about. But just desperately wanting life to be different from what it is creates emotional havoc. Fighting unalterable circumstances is a self-destructive, losing battle; a waste of energy that could be better used to improve life and an incubator for a hostile attitude that pushes good away.

Most successful people have created their own good luck with foresight and perseverance, have painstakingly worked to be in the right places at the right times, and have forged their enviable fates with determination and diligence.

Throwing Away Impractical Demands

Unrealistic expectations are bound to cause discontentment. Whether you anticipate appreciation, help, or love from others or health, wealth, or joy from life, it will not be abundantly supplied simply because you want it. If you allow yourself to be happy only when your wishes are granted and your demands are met, you're setting yourself up for misery and will be forever battling your feelings of having been short-changed.

Expect others to be as they are — true to their own natures and seeking their own pleasures. Then you'll seldom be disappointed in them and feel no need to attempt to extract from them behavior that they cannot or will not display.

If you're not getting what you want from your life, find a way to change it. Be the engineer of your own plan, whether it be to have, to become, or to achieve whatever is your heart's desire, and feel helplessness and hostility fade away. Don't let what you don't have, aren't getting from others, or aren't receiving from life keep you from enjoying what you do have.

Delusions

_____ 7. I will be happy only when ...

I can't be happy because ...

You will be happy only when you, for example, find someone to love, get married, get divorced, get promoted, or have more money. Perhaps you are waiting to be happy at some other time because something is stopping you today — a cast on your broken leg, a chronic health problem, a job you dislike, or a stressful relationship with your spouse, child, or parent. Or you may be unable to be happy now because of regrettable past problems or decisions, such as investing in stock that plummeted or ending a particular relationship.

How are you deluding yourself?

If you are waiting to *really* live sometime in the future, thinking that then things will be different and better, you will never be happy in the present — and that's all you have for sure. Even assuming that you finally reach the goal that promised happiness, much could prevent its realization. Perhaps what you've achieved is no longer what you want or is not what you thought it would be. Maybe reaching another new goal now seems necessary before you can allow yourself to be happy. In the meantime, you've squelched the little daily joys of life by overshadowing them with big dissatisfactions. If you are playing the happiness waiting game, you'll be waiting forever, for all of your tomorrows are bound to be like your todays. If you've decided to live using up the present by anticipating the future, remember — if the path isn't joyful, the destination won't be either.

If you wallow in your past, agonizing over old mistakes, wishing you could relive parts of your life, and kicking yourself for missed opportunities, you are filling your present with discontentment and creating a new past to regret. The past is over; you cannot and need not get it back. Think of past experiences as influences which shaped you into who you are. Savor fond memories, learn from your mistakes, accept your losses, and move on.

You will inevitably waste today if you spend it waiting for or worrying about tomorrow and glorifying or agonizing over yesterday. When tomorrow comes, how will you perceive the yesterday you're creating right now? You're making new memories all the time. Are they wonderful ones or more of the same to feel badly about later?

People who mentally dwell in the past or the future are too distracted from the present to give life the day-to-day attention it requires to be full and gratifying.

_____ 8. I will find personal security by relying on others.

Your security comes from knowing for certain that you can count on someone to provide for you, to take care of you, and to always be there for you. This can be your spouse, girlfriend or boyfriend, parent or child — anyone whom you are counting upon to make you feel secure, provided for, and taken care of.

How are you deluding yourself?

As long as you expect others to give you security, you

are beholden to their wishes, limitations, and moods. Neither marrying and having children nor appealing to another's sense of loyalty or fair play — not even enforcing your "rights" — can guarantee any real security. The only true security comes from realizing that you, yourself, are the most reliable, most logical person upon whom to depend and that you are willing and able to come through for you no matter what comes.

_____ 9. Others are to blame for my troubles and there is nothing that I can do about it.

You think that your life would be fine if it weren't for someone else who is creating problems, such as a meddlesome sister-in-law, jealous lover, or manipulative mother. Such individuals' interference in your life seem to be inevitable and uncontrollable.

How are you deluding yourself?

If you let troublesome individuals intrude in your life, mistreat or misuse you, you alone are responsible for allowing it. You have given them the power to do so. You nearly always have options in the handling of such situations.

But, often, other people are not the true source of one's troubles. Sometimes blaming others is just a way for one to avoid taking responsibility for his or her own shortcomings and errors. It is destructive to hold someone else personally liable for your disappointments, poor judgment, or failures. Doing so prevents you from experiencing the emotional growth which results from facing your own mistakes.

_____ 10. I can't help feeling low much of the time.

Often you feel badly. Perhaps you are worried, frustrated, anxious, upset, irritable, or depressed. Your morale is poor more often than you would like and you feel helpless to improve your usual mental state.

How are you deluding yourself?

Avoiding responsibility for your emotional state leaves you little chance of improving it. You can, indeed, get rid of held-over negative emotions by recognizing them, admitting their existence, expressing them, and dealing with their underlying causes.

___ 11. Everything has a proper place. Every question has an answer. Things are either all one way or all the other and should be done in a certain manner. Change is risky; the old way is best.

You tend to categorize and to divide things and people into carefully constructed, preconceived little cubbyholes. You see most situations as being black or white, good or bad, right or wrong. Usually, once you make a judgment, you close your mind to further evaluation. Often you "all-or-nothing" think yourself into corners from which you must fight your way in order to protect, defend, and reinforce your immovable views. You may cause anxiety in yourself by exaggerating the importance and finality of your decisions.

You live with a routine that you have created, but that you dislike because of the sameness of your world. You are more comfortable limiting experiences and change than in venturing into unknown terrain.

How are you deluding yourself?

Rigidity in thinking and living may seem to provide some degree of emotional security, but, generally, it is responsible for causing more problems than it solves. When one's fixed approach restrains creativity, innovation, and spontaneity, boredom and apathy may result. Tension is also created by an ongoing struggle to get and to keep things sorted out and in their right places and by having to convince oneself and others that they belong there.

Just as palm trees would break and fall in the wind if their trunks were unbending and inflexible, rigid personality frameworks are threatened by pressure against them. Maintaining the integrity of your unyielding personality structure requires continuous effort. Not until you accept that all of life is shades of gray and is ever-changing will you be free to use your precious energy to enjoy life's kaleidoscope of exhilarating experiences.

_____ 12. I *must* fulfill all my obligations to others before doing anything for myself.

Almost every time that you have a choice between doing something for someone else and something for yourself, doing for the other person wins out. Your life may be filled with so many obligations that you seldom have free time to spend as you wish. Sometimes you might even feel somewhat resentful that you are so unselfish.

How are you deluding yourself?

When you consistently put others' needs and desires before your own, you are being unselfish — a highly touted, admirable quality that we have been taught to develop. You feel duty-bound to meet the demands of people. Your life fills up with dreaded activities undertaken to fulfill someone else's selfish self-interest. Then you would like to expect others to put your interests before their own. However, when they do so, *they* resent you; when they don't do so, *you* resent them. You give up your happiness for them and expect them to give up theirs for you. This behavior fosters happiness for no one.

You know best what produces happiness for you and the ultimate responsibility for achieving it is yours. If you create your own happiness by selfishly fulfilling your own needs and desires, the effervescence of your newly found high spirits will spill over onto other people. Doing for them — no longer a drudgery — then becomes a preference. You can be kind, helpful and supportive of others while still looking out for yourself. A certain amount of selfishness is a necessary good — not an evil.

_____ 13. There are very few good, friendly people in this world.

You find most people to be unfriendly, unfeeling, and/or self-seeking. You think that most people are not very nice. They try to get away with whatever they can and, given the chance, would probably take advantage of you.

How are you deluding yourself?

There is an abundant supply of both good and bad all around you. If you look for good, you'll surely find it. If, however, you look for the bad, you'll see it where it is and create it where it isn't. Whichever opposite you focus on will become most apparent. It is easy to get caught up in a pernicious cycle of hostility if you view your world negatively. Those people who have a me-against-the-world attitude walk through life looking for a fight, and they usually get it.

Although today's society necessitates that one be cautious of others in some circumstances, it is self-defeating to allow suspiciousness to invade your approach to people in general. When you do, your unfriendly, possibly harsh, attacking attitude toward others brings out their worst qualities — reinforcing your original opinion that others are untrustworthy or mean and hostile.

Your thoughtful, amicable, positive attitude, however, brings out the best, pleasing, and cooperative side of others — reinforcing your original opinion that others are friendly and caring. Since you have a choice, why not live in a world brimming with good?

Now that you have identified your charisma-blocking beliefs, the next step toward developing Genuine Sustained Charisma is to get rid of these charisma-robbing precepts and their concomitant negative emotions and behaviors. You cannot *will* a lasting change in what you believe or in how you feel or act, as you well know if you have ever unsuccessfully tried to force yourself to do anything — to quit smoking, to diet, or to be happier, for example. Fortunately, there is a more effective way to set free your innate personal magnetism.

Chapter Five

Unblocking Your Charismatic Potential

As long as you keep thinking as you've been thinking, you'll keep feeling as you've been feeling, doing as you've been doing, and getting what you've been getting.

Recently, while waiting in a box-office line to purchase tickets, I overheard two men in front of me as they struck up a conversation. After the first few minutes, the slight, fair-haired one said, "I went to the greatest party last night. The band was fabulous, the singer was terrific, and I met some really interesting people. I stayed until after 2:00 a.m."

In a deep, husky, somewhat perturbed voice, the other man replied, "I should have gone with you last night. I went to a party, too, but what a drag it was! The music was too loud and the people were unfriendly and boring. I got fed up with wasting my time and went home at 9:30."

The two men soon discovered that they had attended the same party.

Hearing this conversation brought to mind a college friend whom I'll call Linda. Last month while shopping, I ran into her after not having seen her since our graduation. We stopped to have a fast lunch so we could catch up with each other's lives.

I had heard through mutual friends that Linda had married and that her husband, Mike, had been seriously injured in a motorcycle accident which had left him partially paralyzed. Still, I was unprepared for what I found. Linda had completely changed from the fun-loving, lively schoolmate of whom I had such wonderful memories into a grim, dejected, bitter woman. She told me that the day they learned Mike was to be forever confined to a wheelchair, she knew that her life was ruined. She no longer could remember what it was like to feel good or to be happy, and she thought she probably never would again.

As I walked out to my car in the parking lot, I couldn't help thinking about my neighbor Pam whose husband, Steven, has Parkinson's disease, causing him to be nearly totally dependent upon her. Although her life is surely difficult in many respects, Pam still loves to play bridge, delights in growing prize roses in her garden, and becomes animated with excitement when their son and his family come to visit from their home in Arizona. And almost always, her sparkling face crinkles with the kind of smile that makes others rejoice in knowing her.

THE MYSTERY OF EMOTIONS AND BEHAVIOR

Why did Linda and Pam, whose husbands both have become disabled, react so differently to their situations? And why did the two men at the box office experience the same party dissimilarly? The answer is that outside events do not directly cause people's emotions or behaviors. It is the beliefs they hold about the events that are responsible.

Your emotional reactions and behaviors may sometimes seem mysterious to you. Possibly nothing is worse than the helplessness which stems from not knowing what causes them and thinking that they are out of your realm of control. Actually, your feelings and actions are explainable, somewhat predictable, and can be quite manageable. You automatically feel and act in accordance with what you believe to be true about yourself and your world. You feel happy or sad and act either in your own best interest or self-defeatingly, depending less upon what actually is than upon your view of it. Your perception of yourself and your world literally creates the reality in which you live. Your life is a projection of your beliefs.

This means that although you may be unable to change your congenital self or existing life circumstances, you can greatly improve your experience of both by transforming any negative, destructive, or counter-productive beliefs you may have about them into positive, constructive, beneficial ones.

A SYSTEM TO CHANGE CHARISMA-BLOCKING BELIEFS

If intellectual recognition of a problem were all that is needed to change how an individual feels and acts, one consultation with a psychologist or psychiatrist would probably be sufficient to "cure" most patients. We know this is not the case. Intellectual realization of the benefit of rejecting a particular belief may be swift, and although emotional and behavioral changes somewhat automatically follow, new modes of thinking can be slow in coming. The emotions are dumb in the sense that they require more time and repetition to accept new information than does the intellect. And just as a change in your thinking results in a change in your behavior, an alteration in your behavior also helps to alter your thinking. How you think, feel, and act are all interdependent. Because each affects the other, the quickest and most effective method of self-change attacks each problem area on all three levels — intellectual, emotional, and behavioral.

I experimented with various ways of accomplishing this and finally settled on a very workable system based primarily on two outstanding psychological philosophies. The first one is Dr. Albert Ellis's Rational-Emotive Therapy which has been extensively researched by behavioral psychologists and is currently used by thousands of mental-health professionals in their treatment of patients. You might recognize the same concepts as being the basis of cognitive and reality therapies. The second philosophy is that of Dr. Maxwell Maltz as espoused in his highly regarded, best-selling book, *Psycho-Cybernetics*.

I recommend that you read Ellis's *A New Guide to Rational Living* and Maltz's *Psycho-Cybernetics*. Both classic texts have been instrumental in improving the lives of many of their readers.

CLEANING OUT YOUR MENTAL CLOSET

You can clean out your head as you would spring-clean a closet. Discard everything that you have outgrown, that you find to be uncomfortable or restrictive and does not show you off to best advantage, or that is not helping you attain the results you want. Substitute new items for each of the old ones until you have a beautiful, fully coordinated wardrobe of beliefs and attitudes that are well-suited to you.

You will feel the excitement of new discoveries, the satisfaction of new understandings, and the awesome relief that comes from releasing yourself from burdensome principles that may have shackled you for as long as you can remember.

As you unclutter your mental closet, you'll become less and less afraid to open yourself up fully to life and to others. And you'll have plenty of room to stock up on the delights and wonders that help to create and nourish that coveted charismatic aura.

Review your old beliefs. Appeal the decision to accept being less than what you want to be or less than what you can be, to get less happiness from life and from others than you want, or to have less than you are capable of attaining.

OUSTING ANTIQUATED CHARISMA-BLOCKING BELIEFS
Reject the belief intellectually.
Step One — Identify the root belief.

If you have an unwanted emotion or behavior which seems to be unrelated to the charisma-blocking beliefs that you already have identified in Chapter Four, trace it back to its underlying assumption by asking yourself *why* you are feeling or acting as you are. Question yourself about any discrepancy between what you think you believe and your actual feelings or actions, trying to expose the idea that is really responsible. Often the ferreted-out belief will contain "should," "shouldn't," "ought," "oughtn't," "must," or "mustn't."

Step Two — Question the rationality of the belief.

Ask yourself if you could be wrong about this belief. Is it based on fact or is it an unfounded assumption? Debate its validity, refuting each point that arises in support of it. Search for inconsistencies and flaws and consider its merit in terms of producing happiness. (You may find it of help to refer to the discussion following each belief in Chapter Four.)

Step Three — Put internal dialogue to work for you.

We all have internal dialogues going on all the time. We may be more aware of them at some times than at others, and some people may notice theirs more than do others, but it is a rote process that we all experience. This self-talk is the basis for how we feel and act. Since it can be interrupted and restructured, dramatic change is possible in our beliefs, attitudes, feelings, and behaviors that, collectively, make up our personalities.

Become aware of what you say to yourself about the undesirable belief. Obstinately refuse to accept any negative or absolutist internal statements. Continually challenge them with reasons why they are inaccurate or exaggerated.

Reject the belief emotionally.

Step Four — Get mad at it.

When you originally acquire a belief, it is an idea that is accompanied by emotion, so it is most effective to employ emotion in its demise. Muster up some indignation that this assumption unnecessarily limited you, perhaps enslaved you, for so long. Work up some stubborn determination to rid yourself of it once and for all.

Step Five — Propagandize yourself.

There is usually a lapse of time between intellectual realization and full emotional acceptance of any concept. This is a critical period best used to indoctrinate yourself against the belief that you are trying to eradicate. You can accomplish this by employing any combination of the following psychological techniques which, by trial and error, you learn works well for you.

Flooding

Drown your mind in an ocean of information by overwhelming it with psychological written material, lectures, workshops, seminars, support groups, motivational tapes — all dealing with general categories, such as self-image psychology and behavior modification, or more specific areas relating to the particular belief you are working on.

Affirmations

Affirmations are positive statements to which you repeatedly expose yourself until they are fully accepted on a subconscious level.

As you remove each charisma-blocking belief from your belief system, it is important to replace it with its positive counterpart. Repeatedly, recite your replacement belief aloud. Make a tape recording of it and listen to it over and over again. Write long lists of the new belief. Make little signs to hang on your bathroom mirror, refrigerator, automobile dashboard, and desk at work — anywhere you will see them often. Combining the concepts of flooding and subliminal suggestion, affirmations can speed reversal of negative beliefs.

Mental Pictures

Because your nervous system cannot tell the difference between a real and a vividly imagined experience, mental pictures can be very helpful in restructuring undesirable attitudes and habitual emotional reactions and behaviors which result from irrational beliefs.

Conjure up a detailed mental motion picture of yourself feeling and behaving as you want in any situation in which your emotions and behavior usually are dictated by a charisma-blocking belief. Repeat this often and your imagined actions and reactions will likely become increasingly evident in your actual experience. This mental practice helps to develop new emotional and behavioral habits just as it improves one's performance of specific skills.

Visualizing works best when you first become relaxed enough to bypass the critical, analytical, judgmental, conscious mind which contributes only 12 percent to one's actual functioning. You can then focus on the feeding of information directly into the more receptive subconscious which is responsible for the remaining 88 percent. To achieve this relaxed state, you might want to experiment with techniques used in self-hypnosis, biofeedback, meditation, or stress management.

Reject the belief behaviorally.

Step Six — Work against it.

Act contrarily to the dictates of your negative belief while maintaining a steady stream of positive, supportive self-talk. Fight any negative thoughts which may try to creep in.

Step Seven — Act "as if."

This well-known technique simply means to behave as if the desired change had already taken place.

Pretend that you are free of your unwanted belief, have fully accepted its positive replacement, and try to feel and act accordingly. Although it will feel artificial at first, continue the new behavior faithfully and it will become increasingly comfortable. Soon, your old behavior will seem strange and foreign; the new one will have become the "new you." Feelings follow actions.

Step Eight — Reward yourself for a job well done.

Congratulate yourself and plan a special treat when you have tried something new, especially difficult, or have achieved a hard-earned success.

YOUR PERSONAL MAP TO
THE EMOTIONAL COMFORT ZONE

Each of your unwanted beliefs may respond best to a different combination of techniques, and, in some cases, all eight steps will not be needed. Some beliefs will seem to change almost miraculously while others will require persistent effort. You will likely find, as have the many others who have used this system, that as you become braver and develop expertise with each successive effort to alter your beliefs, less and less time will be necessary to reach your goals.

Previously, you may not even have realized that your behavior is sometimes irrational. When you first begin working on the charisma-blocking beliefs underlying that behavior, you may find that you become aware of acting inappropriately, but only after the incident is over. Soon, you will be able to recognize such reactions at the time they are happening, but may be unable to control them. The next step is to know what you are doing and to be able to change it while it is in progress. Ultimately, you'll recondition yourself to automatically react properly in previously troublesome situations. Getting rid of your destructive beliefs is a worthy goal — one literally capable of changing your personality.

I remember my own self-confidence building quickly soon after my first couple of successful attempts to modify my beliefs. I boldly set myself up in feared situations almost immediately after identifying my problem, thinking and briefly challenging what I had been telling myself. I began to enjoy the excitement of overcoming my old self-imposed restrictions. As my enthusiasm increased, so did the momentum of my new undertaking. I made a game of sticking my vulnerable little neck out more and more. One by one, many difficulties — ones I had agonized over in the past — just seemed to melt away.

Ultimately, I became free to be myself and discovered that it was fun. In the process, I developed a sense of humor about it all which helped to transform even my most blatant blunders into acceptable, sometimes comical, and occasionally endearing mistakes. I succeeded at tasks that I had previously been afraid to attempt and viewed the inevitable, occasional failures as valuable learning experiences. I realized that magnifying my troubles made them bigger, and that magnifying my joys made *them* bigger, for they were both as I perceived them.

Out of this growth evolved a set of basic concepts which I hold responsible for my continuing celebration of life and usual success with people. Over the years, as I shared these with authors, students, and business and professional clients, they became known as "The Charisma Creed."

THE CHARISMA CREED

Without self-valuations, unrealistic expectations, or delusions, I will try to:

Accept life just as it is — unpredictable, challenging, sometimes trying, but filled with a myriad of opportunities for self-fulfillment.

Accept and like others just as they are — making no attempts to judge, impress, police, control, manipulate, convince, or change them.

Accept, like, trust, be loyal to, depend upon, and believe in myself as I am — ever-changing, learning, growing, getting better.

Be aware of and fulfill my evolving goals and dreams, often reevaluating whether or not my chosen path is still making me happy.

Live and love fully with every ounce of my being, knowing that I may occasionally be hurt, but realizing that that, too, is part of the full experience of living.

Extract from each day and each moment every joyful morsel — remembering the past and planning for the future, but dwelling on only now, today, and how I can make it the best today I've ever known.

When true happiness arrives, true attractiveness is right behind. I wish them both for you.

Chapter Six

Exercising Your Charisma

*When you make the inner you more visible, others
will clamor for your company, delight in your
friendship, and revel in your love.*

An important step toward brightening your personality is to
change those behaviors which impede the flow of your natural
charisma. You may be hiding desirable qualities that would have
great appeal to other people.

At first, attaining the thinking, feeling, and behavioral habits
central to charisma requires persistent effort. With repeated practice, however, these charismatic habits of thinking positively and
living freely, unrestrained by holding-back patterns, become as
automatic as driving your car.

Remember your first time behind the wheel when you thought
you would never be able to steer, signal, watch other cars and traffic lights, operate the accelerator and brake pedals, and still figure
out the best route to get you where you wanted to go? Can't you
now easily do these things and at the same time fix your hair,
change the radio station settings, talk to your passengers, and still
arrive at your destination with almost no conscious thought as
to how you got there? The more experienced you became at driving, the less concentration it required. Being charismatic, too,
becomes an effortless, natural habit when you practice it regularly — a need that can be met by using daily charisma-developing
exercises.

DAILY CHARISMA-DEVELOPING EXERCISES

Because people's existing beliefs, habits, and needs vary widely,
different exercises are necessary for each individual. You can use

any of the following exercises that would serve to bring out your latent charisma, or devise your own. Simply decide in what areas you need to be more positive or more open, and structure an exercise that requires you to experience doing so. These exercises are to be used daily on a temporary basis until whatever you are practicing becomes habitual.

Exercise #1

Make a list of your good qualities and past successes. Read it at least three times a day.

Have you developed a pattern of being very negative about yourself? Most of the time when thinking about yourself, do you remember your mistakes and failures instead of the times you did well? And when you think about the way you look or how you behave, do you focus on the things you don't like rather than the ones you do like?

It is very difficult to feel relaxed and comfortable and to be open with people when you are concentrating on all of the negative aspects of yourself. After all, who wants to expose all that for everyone to see? And if it is what you think about most, it is what you're going to think that others see, too, whether they actually do or not. We all have both flaws and good points. Whichever you choose to dwell on will influence how you feel about yourself and, ultimately, your behavior.

In breaking this habit, it can be helpful to make a list of your good qualities and successful past experiences and to read it frequently. Especially, look it over any time you are thinking negatively about yourself. It will remind you to shift your focus onto your positive qualities.

Exercise #2

Think and speak non-critically for 30 minutes.

Would you be more likely to notice a stranger's attractive smile than his sallow complexion? — the warmth emanating from his or her eyes than that they are small and close together? Looking for things to criticize in others is an extension of being too hard on oneself. Just as focusing on your own shortcomings can prevent you from liking yourself as much as you might and communicating that fact to others, zeroing in on the negative aspects of others can also keep you from projecting the positive "vibes" that are so much a part of charisma.

This exercise can be useful to those who habitually, often unknowingly, criticize themselves and others.

Exercise #3

Do one thing you've been embarrassed to do in the past.

If fears of appearing foolish or inept to others sometimes make you feel uncomfortable or prevent you from attempting challenging new tasks or participating in unfamiliar activities, you could unnecessarily be sacrificing a very likeable part of your personality. Our interest is aroused by people whose unwavering sense of personal security allows them to take emotional risks and to be adventurous.

You can teach yourself how not to feel embarrassed by regularly putting yourself into uncomfortable situations until they no longer cause you to feel self-conscious or ashamed. For instance, you might return a defective product to a store, send back an unsatisfactory meal, ask for help or directions, or eat in an elegant restaurant by yourself. Perhaps you need to practice saying "no" or "I don't care for that." It is important to become practiced at asking for what you want or need and at expressing your preferences.

Training yourself to find humor in your inevitable errors can help to turn even your most awkward experiences into enjoyable ones and you will learn how to sustain the easy confidence typical of charismatic people even in the most difficult situations. If making what seem to be clumsy blunders upsets you, teach yourself how to handle them more confidently by intentionally bumping into a door or turnstile when others are watching, for instance, and encourage yourself not to take it so seriously. In time, even finding your zipper open or having your extended hand ignored will not seriously disturb your sense of emotional security.

Exercise #4

Participate in one childlike activity.

To function well within our society, we have to temper our childlike feelings and behaviors somewhat, but we often carry this process too far by suppressing some of the most attractive qualities of our real inner selves. As we adapt to what others seem to expect, rules, restrictions, and etiquette infiltrate our natural behavior, diminishing simple, wholesome fun; subduing the unabashed thrill of new discoveries; reducing wonderment of our world; constraining unashamed interest in everything and everyone around us; lessening unquestioned trust of our instincts; moderating complete, singular absorption in interesting activities; and restraining spontaneity.

Just as animals know how to be themselves, so do small children — without pretense, defenses, or Emily Post. They are refreshing. They say what they think and do as they feel. Children are in awe of nature's beauty and fearlessly expect the world to be friendly and fun. They give themselves permission to be just as they are — raw, untempered bundles of pure, natural energy. You can recapture some of this quality by decontrolling yourself a little.

Allow yourself to indulge in your penchant for curiosity, to fantasize, to play, or to get silly sometimes. Go up on a swing or down a slide, skip to your mailbox, or roll playfully on the floor with your child. Remember the pure fun of just being you.

As dignity has its place, so romping and frolicking have theirs, for they are reminders of what it feels like to be truly free. Practice being an unadulterated human, filled with an unhampered, genuine love of life and your wealth of effervescence and light-heartedness will greatly enhance your ability to enjoy life and to be found exciting by others.

Exercise #5

Greet at least one new person.

Charismatic individuals automatically make the first overtures toward others. How difficult is it for *you* to approach someone new with a confident smile and a stimulating opening comment? Practicing makes it easier to do and it can greatly improve the response you get from people.

Greet a different person each day. If this prospect creates some anxiety, it might be helpful to decide ahead of time to whom you will speak and plan exactly what you will say to him or her. You might want to begin by choosing someone who is familiar to you — a market-checker or a person who works in the same building as you do, for example. If you feel particularly apprehensive about doing this, first mentally rehearse doing it successfully. Then increase the number of people you approach each day until it becomes comfortable, enjoyable, and habitual.

Other people will find you to be very special when your warm, friendly manner and glowing smile bring an unexpected moment of cheerfulness into their lives.

DAILY CHARISMA-ENHANCING EXERCISES

To stay in tiptop shape, your good, positive feelings require exercise just as your body does. Keep them toned and strong by faithfully using charisma-enhancing exercises. They will help to elevate your spirits and will keep within your field of vision the good things we so often lose sight of. These exercises are for everyone and are to be done on a permanent basis.

Exercise #1

Special day numbers.

Choose a number to take notice of whenever you see it in such places as on license plates, addresses, or the clock. Let it serve as an instant reminder of how lucky you are to have today — a twenty-four-hour opportunity for joy. Be thankful for the gift of life and for the freedom to fill each unretrievable, precious moment of it with calming thoughts and rich experiences. Recognize anew that you are what you make yourself each day and that it is your choice to see either smiles or frowns. Vow to make this day especially enjoyable. Since you will likely see your "chosen number" somewhere at least once each day, you will strive to make *every day* special. Remember, if you do not like today, you probably will never like tomorrow, either.

Exercise #2

Neighborhood reminders.

It is easy to lose your focus on the truly meaningful aspects of your life — to allow momentary difficulties and dissatisfactions to filter them out or to be devoting most of your time to people and activities which contribute the least to your fulfillment.

Pick a familiar neighborhood sight (stoplight, billboard) and every time you see it, bring forth the feelings of vulnerability and finiteness that most of us experience when attending a funeral. And ask yourself, "How and with whom am I spending my limited time?" Vow to see or talk to a favorite person or to do one of your favorite things that day. Plan to do that which has been left undone — place that long-distance call to your mother or straighten out last week's misunderstanding with your longtime friend — for none of us has forever.

Often it takes a heart attack or other close brush with death for a person to reevaluate what really matters to him or her. Don't wait for a crisis to force you to recognize what you've been missing. Live every day as if it's your last while still looking forward to and planning for all your tomorrows.

Exercise #3

Minute vacations.

Mentally kick off your shoes, close your eyes, and just enjoy being alive. When you hurry up to live, you race right past the best of what is worth living for. Instead of running, hurrying, and scurrying through 50 weeks of the year and then trying to cram an entire year's relaxation and enjoyment into a hectic, two-week vacation, take time each day for minute vacations — reflective, joyful moments interspersed throughout your busy daily routine to really see what you are looking at and to appreciate the wonders around you.

Slow down to delight in the fragrance of a blooming flower, in the warmth of a loved one's hug, or in the marvel of a tiny, red ladybug, tickling you as she walks across your hand. Enjoy a lovely moment of peace, feasting on nature's miracles — a rising sun as it illuminates the world or a setting one radiating its colorful tranquility. Feel the excitement of a rainstorm or the freshness of a new snowfall. Spend these moments feeling good about your little place in the natural, grand scheme of things. Realize your miniscule part in the overall picture and the relative insignificance of your day-to-day concerns.

When you let up on your clock-watching, many of life's most elevating sights are yours to experience. The ability to derive real, joyous pleasure from the simple things in life is a mark of an emotionally healthy person with an unfolding potential.

Exercise #4

Mirror friends.

Begin and end every day by looking deeply into the reflection of your own eyes in the mirror and saying, "I love you, (your name)." And every other time you pass a mirror, make eye contact and acknowledge yourself with a quick wink, smile, knowing glance, or wave; and silently or verbally extend a loving greeting to that special friend inside of you. Doing so requires only a few seconds and although it may seem silly, actually it is a very effective method of increasing your self-awareness and self-esteem and of reassuring yourself that you are there for you.

After having done this for years, I am still tickled every time I glance into my own eyes in a mirror and see the special gleam — the unmistakable twinkle that I've come to know so well. It is a moment to joyfully greet and to appreciate the "new me" I've created.

Exercise #5

Evening reflections.

Each night just before going to sleep, rather than thinking about your problems and the things that went wrong that day or that are waiting for you to do the following day, take a few minutes to recall and savor that day's most enjoyable moments, or read passages from an inspirational book. At this particular time, there is an intricate interplay between your conscious and subconscious minds. If you spend these moments thinking about the most happy, fulfilling parts of your day or focusing on lovely thoughts, the positive feelings tend to be long-lasting.

CHARISMA-SUSTAINING BEHAVIORS

The following basic behaviors are critical to expanding and perpetuating the charismatic spirit.

Behavior #1

Develop a treasured self-friendship.

The one to whom you are the very closest, with whom you will inevitably spend your entire life, sharing joys and sorrows, successes and failures, good and poor health, and will be unable to ever become angry or bored enough with to separate from is *yourself.* Although you have to maintain a lifelong relationship, you may not be treating yourself with as much respect and concern as you would a mere acquaintance.

How you see, feel about, and treat yourself are of paramount importance for they determine how you will experience life and how others will perceive you. Your self-image can be an interference or an enhancement to your personal satisfaction and performance. There is a person inside you whom you can develop to always be there for you, someone you can always count on to see you through your worst moments and to share in your best ones. No other relationship can do for you what a satisfying self-relationship can. Make yourself your first friend, and others will follow. Cultivate a friendship with your inner person by:

Treating yourself kindly, politely, and caringly.

This means no name-calling, labeling, insulting, belittling, or unproductive criticizing. If you are not treating yourself nicely, you can forget trying to change because change occurs in a warm, accepting emotional climate. As long as you are fighting yourself, you will be waging an internal battle that you are constantly fueling. To change, you need the help of that little friend within you. Treat your inner person as you would anyone whose help you are eliciting, or it will sabotage your best efforts to change yourself or to succeed. Your goal is to feel good about yourself so you can grow and change — not to change so you can feel good about yourself.

Giving yourself the benefit of the doubt.

Do not be forever looking for flaws and errors to emphasize or be quick to blame yourself when something goes wrong. Dwell on your likeable qualities and forgive yourself your shortcomings. By nature's criteria, you are perfect as you are. You aren't meant to be flawless and if you aren't making mistakes, you aren't alive.

Being supportive of yourself when tackling
new and difficult tasks or situations.

In order to feel free to open up emotionally to others, we need to know that it is safe to do so. The most effective way to build an unshakeably secure foundation on which to base our approach to others is to be getting all the support we need from ourselves. When we know that a deep part of ourselves is unquestionably there to support us, we develop the security necessary to take the emotional risks with others that are so often attractive.

It is easy to be supportive of yourself when everything is going great and you are doing terrifically well. But if you can do it when things are not so good — that is when you'll know you have a real friend. And immediately praise yourself for a job well done, a new emotional risk taken, or a situation well-handled, just as you would like for a best friend to do.

Build your inner security and confidence by reminding yourself that you are there for you no matter what comes and that you will lovingly make it together.

Being true to your values.

Self-respect stems from being faithful to the precepts of highest priority to you — by following what you think is right regardless of how others may perceive your decisions.

Developing your camaraderie.

Enjoy inside jokes and secrets that you share only with yourself. Develop private expressions meaningful only to you. Appreciate your idiosyncrasies and learn to laugh and to have fun with yourself. Whenever possible, sing to yourself — while driving in your car or getting dressed, for example. These things help you to build with yourself a close, personal relationship that you would value were it to be with someone else.

Pleasuring yourself.

Our charisma is tied to our ability to give and to partake of pleasure. Do you get enough to sustain and to nourish you? Pleasure affirms life and provides needed energy for self-creation.

In my charisma classes, I always ask the students, "How many chocolate-cake lovers do we have in here who save the frosting for last?" Those individuals who raise their hands usually have a "save-the-pleasure-for-later" mind-set that permeates their entire lives. They are the ones who save things for special occasions instead of enjoying them at the time the opportunity arises. I have had such students call me sometime later and say that they found it liberating to allow themselves to enjoy their pleasures at the height of their desire for them and that they had never before thought of choosing to do so.

When you save the best for last, it sometimes is disappointing or doesn't come at all. There is no guarantee that you are going to be able to enjoy it later. Don't wait for special occasions to wear your good jewelry, your most flattering outfit, or your best cologne. Feel special every day by luxuriating in your favorite things.

Behavior #2

Get the happiness habit.

Creating happiness within yourself is a wonderful habit to cultivate. When in a good frame of mind, you are a delight to yourself and a bright spot in the lives of those around you. Although it is not always desirable or even reasonable to be at the top of the exuberance scale, getting up there frequently serves as a good reminder of what pure, true happiness feels like and makes it easier to reproduce at varying degrees. Like a singer stretching his or her voice range, a happiness-seeker can learn through experience and practice to climb the scale easily and to achieve a richer, fuller end result.

An actor can create a particular emotion in himself by concentrating on thoughts which bring forth the desired reaction. Knowing that he cannot command emotions, he does not order himself to feel happy, for example. Instead, he mentally recalls or reenacts an experience he remembers brought him great joy, and soon there it is — the happiness envelops him just as it did the first time. He can then enhance the feelings by becoming acutely aware of what all his senses tell him happiness feels like and by focusing on those sensations. He can also bring back the original feeling of happiness at a later time by reproducing the recalled physical feelings associated with it. It literally requires less and less effort to feel happy and to upgrade it to happier, happiest when this technique is used. Sports psychologists use it extensively with athletes to help them get "psyched up" before playing a game or entering a competition.

You can use the same technique to produce or to enhance your own good feelings. You create your own emotions all the time in much the same way as do the actors and athletes, but you are usually unaware of the process.

You cannot be cheerful if you concentrate on negatives, and misery is difficult, if not impossible, to produce when you think positively. The low morale which is so common among otherwise emotionally healthy people is often simply a result of gloomy thinking.

All of us at some time must deal with troublesome problems and stressful situations. At other times, we feel marvelous with no effort. The thoughts we let pitter-patter through our minds during the remaining "uncommitted" periods will determine how much actual time we spend feeling happy.

We are what we think about all day long. What do you fill your mind with when there are no immediate, pressing issues demanding your attention? Are you thinking about how many bills you have stacked up waiting to be paid, how far behind you are in your work, or how dissatisfied you are with your social life, or agonizing over your flaws and shortcomings? If so, you are keeping your spirits down all the time that you are dwelling upon these non-productive, negative thoughts. And when you are feeling low, you look it.

Have you ever noticed people's faces in other cars while stopped at a red light? What did you see? Mostly frowns and looks of preoccupied concern, anger, frustration, or sadness? All too often we project pain and ugliness to others. Charismatic individuals do not drive others away by throwing such emotional daggers at them. Being charismatic requires that you have a warm, inviting, friendly face — one you will not have while thinking negatively.

So the next time you are standing in line at the post office, waiting for a bus, or daydreaming while idling your car at a red light, become aware of your inner dialogue. If it is negative, visualize a big, bright red stop sign. Then picture a broom sweeping away the negative clutter. Replace this with the mental image of something that brings you great pleasure. It may be your child, a favorite vacation spot, or simply a bouquet of flowers. When this image fades, be sure to allow only positive thoughts to replace it. Because the negative side in each of us is stronger and more practiced than the positive side, at first you will need to forcibly and repeatedly push out negative thoughts and replace them with positive ones. In time, by feeding yourself positive thoughts, you can unlearn negative thinking patterns and teach yourself to get the happiness habit.

Behavior #3

Be an energy.

We rarely find a passive person charismatic. We clamor to get within striking distance of the positive energy the charismatic personality expends so freely. There is an undefineable magnetism in this projected human energy. It is that extra spark that says, "I've got what it takes." It is shared as enthusiasm — that compelling mental attitude that comes from the heart and is as enduring as faith and courage. It attracts people, makes them eager to help you, and removes even the most difficult obstacles to fulfillment and success. Everyone has this energy source deep within themselves but many people block its unrestrained expression. Learning how to generate and control it is one of the most important keys to developing your charisma.

You can feel more fully alive and communicate that excitement to others by getting into life. Strong conviction about, belief in, and dedication to whatever you do creates enthusiasm in yourself that stimulates others. And the energy produced by giving everything your best effort can make any task exhilarating — whether it be mopping a floor, washing your car, singing a song, or closing a business deal. Charismatic individuals are doers and they can move others to action. Their enthusiasm is highly contagious.

If you feel sapped by apathy and boredom or just find life to be rather dull, try to decide what you really want and formulate a plan to get it. Discovering what moves you and working toward attaining it will give your life direction, inspire confidence, and create boundless enthusiasm for living. Set goals that allow you to stretch yourself. Spend more time as a participant and less as a spectator. Propel yourself into challenges at work and at play. Become absorbed in creative endeavors by feeding your creative instincts with new ideas and exposing yourself to new adventures and experiences. And act enthusiastic. Once generated, enthusiasm tends to help perpetuate itself.

Behavior #4

Go for the brass ring.

In life, just as on an old-time carousel pony, you can catch the brass ring only if you stretch high enough to reach it. By so doing, you could fall before reaching the rings, you might succeed at getting one that was not brass, or you might catch the brass ring that entitles you to a free ride. Some individuals choose not to risk trying. They sit securely going around and around, perhaps initially enjoying the scenery, but then, most likely, enduring the inevitable boredom. But where is the fun, the challenge, the sense of accomplishment, the variety, and the growth?

Many people expend a great deal of effort maintaining their bland existences at a steady, stable, safe level. Anything or anyone who threatens to rock their boat is cast away. They are probably successful in avoiding some pain and some lows, but they forfeit their highs in the process. In a sense, emotions are a package deal. If you hold back in one area, you will automatically do so in another. If you do not open yourself up because you are afraid to risk possible discomfort, you will not be able to take in the full range of enjoyments either. You will be as inaccessible to good as you are to bad. Just as there can be no ups without downs or tops without bottoms, there perhaps can be no happiness without sadness or pleasure without pain. It is all a natural part of living. At times, we have all been hurt, but we did not wither or die. Somehow we survived until the distress passed, as it nearly always seems to do.

Pain gives one emotional depth which can be used to fully experience pleasure. Risk living passionately and feeling life deeply. Be able to cry for a stranger's pain and rejoice in his or her good fortune. People who venture whatever it takes to live fully, come to know the true worth of being alive. And the excitement and joy they exude attracts others who want to be able to do it, too, and who want to be part of the fun, of the excitement, and of the exhilaration. When you are the one who "goes for it," you are giving people something they probably aren't getting anywhere else.

Behavior #5

Fulfill your fondest dreams.

There is no such thing as a fully fulfilled person. Everybody has some form of unfulfilled desire. Which of *your* dreams got lost in the shuffle of growing to maturity? Are any of them salvageable? Did you want desperately to be a dancer, master chef, or an actor? Have you wished you could play a musical instrument, stain glass, or ice skate? Perhaps your mind often wishfully wanders off to the same unrealized dream or unmet goal. Wishful thoughts are messages from your inner self. You can help to develop your true charismatic personality by reaching out for your deepest desires.

Become aware of what your inner person yearns for. You cannot fulfill unrecognized dreams, achieve unknown goals, or enjoy unidentified pleasures. You have to learn what you want before you can execute a plan to get it. What would you be regretful about having missed or not having done were you to have only a very short time left to live? These are the activities with which to fill your days now while you still have the chance.

How many people find that they are either too old or too ill to do the things they wanted to do? They were waiting for the right time to pursue their dreams, but when is the right time — when you are twenty, forty, sixty, eighty or older? As long as you have a reason for not doing it today, you'll likely have a reason every day. You may never actualize your fondest dreams unless you begin now. Start today to turn your dreams into attainable goals by formulating a plan to achieve them and acting upon it. The energy that you generate will spill over and positively affect your relationships with other people. And the satisfaction you will derive upon finally making your longtime dreams come true will be indescribably delicious!

Behavior #6

Surround yourself with positive thinkers, inspirational books, happy music, and humor.

Your present personality is largely a result of your past psychological environment. And the person you will become depends upon your present and future environment. The people in your life are mirrors of you. They reflect aspects of your personality. What kind of people surround you? Are they negative? If so, your negativism is showing. If they are cynical, your cynicism is showing. Not only do we seek out those who are like us, but our minds absorb and reflect what they see. If you have prolonged associations with negative people, you will likely continue to think negatively, too. Choose friends who are positive, who sincerely want to see you succeed, and who are enthusiastic about and encourage you in your pursuits. Guard your psychological environment from pettiness, gossip, and jealousy. Limit the amount of time you will allow negative input — whether it be from the mass media, from other people's conversations, or from your own thoughts.

Get plenty of psychological sunshine to brighten your personality. Institute a regular reading program of inspirational and motivational books. They make almost anything seem possible. A steady diet of their "you-can-do-it" philosophy helps to balance our negatively-weighted environment.

Music is a therapeutic emotional treatment. It can seduce you into a state of flow — of total involvement that produces a calm or a high that releases you from your usual emotional restrictions. It helps you to experience your emotions more intensely. Happy music can turn an okay mood into a great one. Get into the habit of listening whenever you can — while getting dressed, eating, or riding in your car.

Laugh a little bit every day. Humor helps the body to heal itself, the mind to rejuvenate itself, and the soul to soar. Regularly expose yourself to the light side of life by reading humorous books, watching funny movies, and listening to amusing records or to jokes. Learn to make fun wherever possible by looking for the humor in everyday situations.

Make every effort to insure that your exposure to the positive outweighs that of the negative, and you will be well rewarded.

Your life can be a symphony of beautiful melodies or a succession of unharmonious notes. The choice is ultimately yours, for you compose your own music each and every day.

Chapter Seven

How to Create and Sustain a Charismatic Aura

*Strong personal magnetism grows out of
nourishing other people's good feelings,
especially about themselves.*

Freeing our real inner selves, becoming more adept at experiencing and expressing happiness, cultivating a positive outlook based on a healthy, deep-seated philosophical system, and having an energetic, enthusiastic approach to life are important prerequisites to developing a charismatic aura. But to actually radiate charisma that will magnetically attract people and will sustain that attraction and cause it to grow, we also need to act charismatically toward others minute by minute and day by day. How we present ourselves and how we treat people greatly affect how we are perceived.

WHAT IS YOUR BEHAVIORAL STYLE?

Everyone develops a certain manner of approaching others in hopes that it will win their approval and acceptance. But often, we are unaware of what our approach is and how it affects them. It may be ineffective or, worse, it may even repel some people.

Identify your own behavioral style and determine whether you are receiving the response you want. Are you the all-knowing, infallible type who has an answer for everything? Or do you seem cool, aloof, blasé, and unemotional, appearing to need no one? Perhaps you have an air of superiority or use sexual seductiveness or helplessness in an attempt to win over others. Do you try to impress them with your education, accomplishments, or money? Or to make them feel sorry for you or make allowances for you

because of illness or a streak of bad luck? Maybe you try to be
the kind of person others seem to want, agreeing with everything.
Do you laugh too much or flatter too easily?

We don't like insincere individuals nor those who build themselves
up at our expense by putting us down. The showoff, the braggart,
and the arrogant person who try to make others feel inferior are
usually suffering from low self-esteem which keeps them from being themselves. They don't believe that they are good, interesting,
or lovable enough to gain the approval and admiration they need,
so they hide their true selves behind facades they believe will be
more likely to produce the results they want. And they use these
facades as protective devices in an effort to shield their vulnerable
egos from the rejection they fear will result from exposing their
real selves to others.

The shy person also has low self-esteem but usually physically
avoids or emotionally withdraws from interpersonal situations
which cause him or her to be ill at ease.

Truly charismatic individuals are neither too reserved nor too
over-bearing. They are not passive, tense, or aggressive. Instead,
they have sufficient self-esteem to approach others directly and
honestly, for they do not live in constant fear of their negative
evaluations. If this fear causes you to camouflage your true self,
you are disguising one of your strongest sources of appeal — the
natural charm that comes from being yourself.

INTO EVERY LIFE SOME REJECTION MUST FALL

Everyone faces rejection at some time in his or her life. The
most successful salespeople cannot close 100 percent of the sales
they attempt. Major corporations make billions of dollars selling
their products to as few as 2 percent of the population. This means
that 98 percent of the people do not use their products. Millions
of people voted against our President while millions of others
elected him to the highest office in our nation. Actors star in box-
office flops, job applicants get turned down, and offers of friendship are refused.

Life is not a popularity contest. Recognize that it is impossible
for you to be what everyone wants because each individual wants
something different depending upon his or her own needs and
desires. Become confident in who you are and open up to others

knowing that those whom you attract are interested in and are likely to appreciate what you have to offer. We seek out people who are like us — those with whom we have common interests, values, philosophies, and who complement our own strengths and weaknesses. We receive no long-range satisfaction or fulfillment from attracting those who like us only for what we pretend to be.

Accept some rejection as being inevitable and know that it does not mean that you are unworthy, inferior, or undesirable; it is merely an expression of someone else's prejudices and preferences.

FROM SELF-CONSCIOUSNESS TO SELF-CONFIDENCE

Five of us were standing together talking at a cocktail party, when one of the women, Helen, began to choke on an hors d'oeuvre. Her face became contorted as she struggled to breathe. The moment the episode ended, she ran to the ladies' room, saying she wanted to fix her tear-smeared eye make up. My friend Suzanne and I followed her to make sure that she was all right. We found her crying and attempted to calm her down, assuming that she was frightened by the incident. But all she said was, "How did I look? I must have looked awful! I'm too embarrassed to go back out there."

It took Suzanne and me half an hour to convince Helen that people were concerned only about her welfare and that the only one who thought about how she appeared while choking was herself.

People are seldom as observant as self-conscious individuals imagine them to be. Nor are they as critical as a self-conscious person is of himself or herself.

I attended a wedding recently at which the groom's mother had a broken leg. She was determined to sit out the reception so that she could keep her cast hidden under the table. She had decided to trade the fun of fully participating in her only son's wedding celebration for the safety of "not looking awkward."

Self-conscious people miss some of the potentially most rewarding experiences of life because of their fear about how they may appear to others. Self-consciousness results from being too concerned about "what others think." People's sensitivity to disapproval in others causes them to constantly and consciously monitor everything they say or do, inhibiting the spontaneous, easy manner typical of charismatic individuals.

People accept you as you accept yourself. Work to feel good about yourself as you are and to develop confidence in what you have to offer, and you will feel less anxious about gaining acceptance. No longer preoccupied with yourself and what others are thinking about you, you will be free to focus, instead, upon other people. When you direct your attention to understanding and loving those around you rather than expecting them to understand and love you, a wonderful transformation will take place in their response to you. People are most impressed by those who show interest in *them*. An irresistible charm arises out of your awareness of others and their needs and desires. The more you know about what motivates them, the more likely you will attract them and sustain that attraction.

HOW TO CAPTURE THE INTEREST OF OTHER PEOPLE

Though people differ greatly in attitude, goals, and lifestyles, they share many of the same basic psychological needs. One of our strongest psychological needs is for self-esteem. Every person wants desperately to be noticed, accepted, praised, and appreciated. We all want to feel special and important. Charismatic individuals are thought to be attractive and desirable because, in part, they routinely satisfy these universal human hungers in others. They know how to make people feel good about themselves. And you can do it, too, by learning how to approach others with a charismatic attitude.

HOW TO DEVELOP A CHARISMATIC ATTITUDE

Shine a spotlight on everyone.

Treat every individual with equal respect, interest, and concern — whether he or she is your building's maintenance person or your boss, a counter person at your dry cleaners or an important new client.

Many of the people whose paths we cross in our daily lives are accustomed to being ignored or treated poorly. Every bank teller, salesperson, and waitress or waiter has concerns, goals, and dreams. Each one of them gets up and goes about the sometimes tedious business of living each day, just as you do. Make the most of every opportunity to "connect" with others by being interested in them, by caring, and by letting it show.

These people will become happy to see you. You will likely be greeted with a smile, with a hello, and maybe with your name. They will put forth extra effort to serve you politely and efficiently. Many will be eager to do extra things for you. They will treat you as a special person — because you are acting like one. Errands and chores will become especially enjoyable as you begin to view them as chances to experience others and to have them experience you.

Put others at ease.

We like to be with people who make us feel comfortable. You can bring out the best in others by giving them an opportunity to open up, to be themselves, and to feel good about doing so. They will associate with you the good feelings they have about themselves.

Notice each person's behavioral style. Don't be intimidated by those who come on strongly. Recognize bragging and "lording-it-over-you" behavior for what it is — a meek attempt by a tiny, insecure, struggling ego for acceptance, approval, and protection from potential outside threats. People who behave in this way are usually trying to convince themselves of their own worth. Both overbearing and shy people need to feel themselves in an emotionally safe environment to take the risk of dropping their postures and pretenses.

You can give others the gift of sharing and feeling good about their real selves by helping them to focus on their strengths and attributes and by accepting and showing approval of them as individuals without judging, comparing, or competing. There is tremendous personal power in responding to what is going on under the surface of others' behaviors.

I remember one time, in particular, when I didn't take my own advice. I was, for the first time, meeting a man I'll call Dr. David Rodell and his wife who was also a doctor. He was the speaker at an informal exercise/lecture/demonstration. When introduced to him, I said, "How do you do, David?" His wife replied, "His name is Dr. Rodell and, for that matter, so is mine."

He appeared to be very embarrassed and several people who were standing nearby were visibly shaken by her rude outburst. You could hear the dead silence as everyone waited for my reply.

"Oh, I'm also a doctor," I said. She asked, "In what field?" With a straight expression on my face and looking her right in the eyes, I replied, "I'm a brain surgeon." And I walked away feeling happy and satisfied.

Knowing that this woman's security at that moment was dependent upon establishment of her status and "superiority," it would have been far preferable for me to have smilingly said, "How very nice to meet you both, Dr. Rodell and Dr. Rodell." I hadn't been charismatic and hadn't cared to be. She just rubbed me the wrong way. Well, no one's perfect!

Help others to value themselves more.

When you show genuine interest in someone and are considerate and appreciative, you tend to increase that person's feelings of self-worth, indirectly causing him or her to think well of you. We want to like people who like us. And we want to think of them as being perceptive and as having good taste.

Find positive things to like in people and let them know about them. Give praise for subtle virtues you observe that others don't readily see. And pay honestly earned compliments freely.

Show others you value them by being polite, by immediately acknowledging their presence, by being on time, and, whenever appropriate, by thanking them for their effort, thoughtfulness, time, or care. Ask for their advice and suggestions. Doing so makes people feel important and lets them know that you respect their opinions. When someone impresses you, show it. And giving credit where it is due allows you to increase another's sense of satisfaction and accomplishment.

Last summer, a group of us who had been friends at college reunited to "catch up" on each other's lives. We exchanged the usual questions, one of which was, "What do you do?" — to which one woman, Jennifer, replied dejectedly, "I'm only a secretary."

"What do you mean by *only* a secretary?" Norma asked. "I used to do office work and found it to be challenging and satisfying."

Feeling better about her job, Jennifer then began to relate her most rewarding work experience.

Norma knew what we would do well to remember — that every type of honest work has honor and that it feels wonderful to help others take pride in what they do.

Become a messenger of happiness.

Mounted on the wall in my office is a column by Art Buchwald that appeared in the *Los Angeles Times*. It clearly captures the spirit of a charismatic person in action.

Art Buchwald

WATCH HIM! HE COULD BE CONTAGIOUS!

I was in New York recently and took a ride with a friend of mine in a taxi. When we got out of the cab, my friend said to the driver, "Thank you for the ride. You did a superb job of driving."

The taxi driver was stunned for a second. Then he said, "Are you a wise guy or something?"

"No, my dear man, and I'm not putting you on. I admire the way you keep your cool in heavy traffic."

"Yeh," the driver said and drove off.

"What was that all about?" I asked.

"I am trying to bring love back to New York," he said. "I believe it's the only thing that can save the city."

□

"How can one man save New York?"

"It's not one man. I believe I have made that taxi driver's day. Suppose he has 20 fares. He's going to be nice to those 20 fares because someone was nice to him. Those fares in turn will be kinder to their employees or shopkeepers or waiters or even their own families. They, in turn, will be nicer to other people. Eventually the good will could spread to at least a thousand people. Now that isn't bad, is it?"

"But you're depending on that taxi driver to pass your good will to others."

"I'm not depending on it," my friend said. "I'm aware that the system isn't foolproof. I might deal with 10 different people today. If, out of 10, I can make three happy, then eventually I can indirectly influence the attitudes of 3,000 more."

"It sounds good on paper," I admitted, "but I'm not sure it works in practice."

"Nothing is lost if it doesn't. It didn't take any of my time to tell that man he was doing a good job. He neither received a larger tip nor a smaller one. If it fell on deaf ears, so what? Tomorrow there will be another taxi driver I can try to make happy."

"You're some kind of a nut," I said.

"That shows you how cynical you have become. I have made a study of this. The thing that seems to be lacking, besides money of course, for our postal employees is that no one tells people who work for the post office what a good job they're doing."

"But they're not doing a good job."

"They're not doing a good job because they feel no one cares if they do or not. Why shouldn't someone say a kind word to them?"

☐

We were walking past a structure in the process of being built and passed five workmen eating their lunches. My friend stopped. "That's a magnificent job you men have done. It must be difficult and dangerous work."

The five men eyed my friend suspiciously.

"When will it be finished?"

"October" a man grunted.

"Ah! That really is impressive. You must all be very proud."

We walked away. I said to him, "I haven't seen anyone like you since 'The Man of La Mancha.' "

"When those men digest my words, they will feel better for it. Somehow the city will benefit from their happiness."

"But you can't do this all alone!" I protested. "You're just one man."

"The most important thing is not to get discouraged. Making people in the city become kind again is not an easy job, but if I can enlist other people in my campaign..."

"You just winked at a very plain-looking woman," I said.

"Yes, I know," he replied. "And if she's a schoolteacher, her class will be in for a fantastic day."

Reprinted with permission of the author

Develop a gaiety of spirit and share it freely. It is one of the true joys of living and brings rewards beyond description. Nice people attract nice things.

Be considerate of people's feelings.

We are all sensitive and can be easily hurt by harsh or thoughtless comments or acts.

While having dinner at a neighborhood restaurant, I overheard several young men joking with their little blond waitress. She seemed to be enjoying their attentions and returned frequently to check on the progress of their meal. Just before they left, one of the men asked her, "What are you doing after work?" She replied, "I'm going home to my husband. Can't you see this ring? I'm married!"

Wouldn't it have been far more considerate of the young man's feelings for the waitress to have thanked him for his interest and to have said that had she not been married, she would have been tempted by his invitation? Does it hurt to help another to save face? Make an effort to do and say what you would want done and said were you in the other person's position.

Once, when a friend excitedly told a group of us that she was planning a trip to Morocco, someone said, "That's the *last* place in the world *I* would ever choose to go!"

Not only does such a remark diminish the joy of the person who is sharing something special, but it is detrimental to the image of the individual who is unkind enough to make it. There is no excuse for ever taking the chance of hurting another person's feelings in this manner. Think before you say things that might cause pain to others. A charismatic person is kind in thought, word, and deed.

Go out of your way to be nice.

Have you ever offered to let someone with only a few items to purchase go before you in a grocery line? Do you routinely hold doors open for people entering stores behind you?

Charismatic individuals are people-lovers who derive great satisfaction from "going that extra mile" for others.

I have experienced innumerable instances of people putting themselves out for me, and each time I have thought of them as being very special individuals.

I remember one cold, winter evening when I was struggling to carry a briefcase and two boxes of books across a college campus to the building where I was scheduled to teach a class. I sat resting briefly for the second time on a concrete retaining wall with my

arms and shoulders aching and wondering how I would ever get
my supplies to my second-floor classroom in a still-distant building.
A young man came up to me and said I looked as if I needed
help. And then he proceeded to carry my books all the way to
my classroom door.

Recently, I broke my foot while vacationing alone in a small
town nearly 100 miles northeast of Los Angeles. Unable to drive
home wearing the splint the emergency room physician had put
on my right foot, I sat in the hotel lobby trying to decide how
to get home. Three hotel guests came up to me, one by one, offering to interrupt their vacations to drive me back to Los Angeles.
And two hotel employees also said they would drive me home if
I could wait until they got off work. I declined their help, opting
instead to take the suggestion of another concerned guest who
recommended that I employ a limousine service. More than half
a dozen genuinely empathetic people lined up to hug me goodbye
and to wish me a speedy recovery.

Since then, I have been able to get around with my cast and
crutches and to run some of my errands, thanks to the many individuals who have helped me in and out of my car in parking
lots, have carried bundles from stores, and have come to my aid
in a variety of other ways.

We all have dozens of opportunities each day to do a little
something extra for others. When these chances arise, are you nice
or not so nice? Try to recall the last time someone smiled ap-
preciatively at you and gave you a warm "thank you" for something
you did. Was it yesterday, last week, or last month? Does it happen frequently?

Charismatic individuals are nice every day to every person, no
matter what the situation. This does not mean that they allow
themselves to be used, taken advantage of, or taken for granted;
rather, that they look out for their own interests and maintain their
own standards of integrity but are mindful of the needs and sensitivities of other people.

WHAT YOUR AUTO PERSONALITY SAYS ABOUT YOU

Very often the way a person drives is the way he or she lives.
Driving behavior can be a microcosm of an individual's approach
to life in general.

Do you relax and enjoy the sights as you drive or do you race from one red signal to the next, forever intent upon getting to your destination? Do you notice and smile at other drivers or are you in a private world all your own, oblivious of everyone and everything around you?

The existence or absence of niceness, too, is evident in one's driving habits. The nice person signals his or her intent to turn left in plenty of time for followers to change lanes if they desire. And he or she does not plow through puddles, splashing water and mud on other cars, especially if another car is carefully maneuvering through a wet spot to avoid getting dirty. Nor does a nice person mindlessly barrel through puddles, drenching pedestrians. He or she smilingly waves others in front of himself or herself at such places as freeway on-ramps and lane-closed areas. The person who won't let you into the flow of traffic, who will squeeze you onto a shoulder or into a ditch in order to stay in front, is usually not a friendly, considerate, nice person anywhere outside his or her automobile any more than inside. Happy, fulfilled people who like themselves and others do not need to "beat out" the other guy. And an individual who steals your parking spot most likely takes a "me-first" attitude in other areas of his or her life, too.

Being nice to other drivers on the road makes you feel good about yourself and affirms your belief in the niceness of others. Most people will appreciate your considerate treatment of them and will smile and wave to thank you. Being nice becomes habitual as you practice it and tends to carry over into other areas of your life.

MODERN ETIQUETTE AND OLD-FASHIONED MANNERS

Many people are fed up with the rudeness that is rampant in America, from curt salespersons and ill-mannered customers to disrespectful children, tactless friends, and surly strangers.

Until recently, the hippie movement of the 1960s and the "me" generation of the 1970s had left us with a lingering unconcern for the welfare of others. But the pendulum is swinging back. There is now an unprecedented interest in courtesy and good manners. Etiquette writers and consultants are in great demand as formality once again is in style. But manners are being brought back differently. Modern etiquette addresses everything from corporate and computer manners to the propriety of having a lover stay overnight when your roommate is home. The "right" way to act is often controversial as we live in a time when what is polite to one person may be rude to another. But good manners are a reflection of good character. And although the rules are changing, being nice to other people is still what manners are all about. Simple courtesies indicate that we care. And they are necessary to succeed in both our work and personal lives.

HOW TO HAVE SOCIAL CONFIDENCE

To be charismatic, an individual must feel confident that he or she knows the right thing to do in various situations and is capable of following through. When self-doubt creeps in, the positive energy that feeds the charismatic aura diminishes noticeably.

New guidelines require us to define the context in which we find ourselves and to be flexible in our responses. It is important to consider with whom you are dealing and under what circumstances. There may be no correct way to deal with a particular situation. Determine the nicest way you can handle it that is consistent with your values and sense of self.

Let consideration for the other person be your guideline rather than being preoccupied with your own rights. When someone is rude to you, don't stoop to his or her level by responding in an equally rude manner. Doing so will be far more destructive to you than to the other person.

WHAT TO DO ABOUT DOORS, COATS, CHECKS, AND SMOKING

Such acts as opening doors and holding coats are courtesies appropriate to both sexes. One should use common sense as the basic criterion for deciding what is and what is not acceptable. Ordinarily, whoever gets to a door first should open it. A woman who observes a man burdened with packages heading for a door, should open it for him just as he should for her if their positions were reversed.

It is correct and thoughtful for anyone, male or female, to hold a coat for someone who is trying to put one on and to pay the check if he or she did the inviting. The guiding rule is to do whatever is natural and comfortable for you and for the other person.

When you do not know another person well enough to judge what behavior he or she would prefer in a particular situation, feel free to ask. For instance, a man may ask a woman he is with, "May I help you with your coat?" If she does not want him to assist her, she can simply say, "No, thank you."

And do not hesitate to express your behavioral preferences. The first time I rode in a certain male friend's automobile, I opened the passenger door and got out immediately upon arriving at our destination. He commented that he thought it was terrific that women's roles have changed and that they have become self-sufficient in many new ways but that he has, for a lifetime, opened doors for his female companions and considers doing so a way of showing them he feels they are special. If it was all right with me, he said, he would prefer to open the car door for me rather than to have me do it myself.

Some men feel uncomfortable unless they open doors, hold coats, and pay checks for women. If you are a woman in the company of such a man, let him extend these niceties even if you feel a bit awkward about it. All such gestures are expressions of another person's upbringing and/or respectful, considerate, caring attitude toward you — and that is all they are. Too often we regard them as political or sociological statements.

Besides personal preferences, what is appropriate is somewhat dictated by the formality of any situation. Generally, the more formal the occasion, the more traditional the manners.

The 1980s may prove historically to be the decade of the smokers versus the non-smokers. But knowing who is imposing upon whom need not create animosity between people. You should not ask someone to refrain from smoking in his or her own home or office, but you can make such request in *your* home or office. If you are a non-smoker and are asked by a smoker whether or not you mind if he or she smokes, feel free to say yes, remembering to thank that person for asking. Politeness and consideration of the other person's rights are always in fashion.

We all make occasional social errors, but knowing what to do becomes easier as you experience handling a variety of situations. So don't be afraid of not knowing all the rules. I once read that Emily Post's only real qualification was that she had attended a lot of parties. Haven't you attended a lot of parties, too?

HOW TO MAKE CHARISMA LAST

To achieve charisma that will last far beyond the first few minutes of a new acquaintanceship and make us special and memorable to others, we must work to develop the deep, sensitive, compassionate parts of ourselves, to routinely treat others gently and affectionately, to be aware of their motivations, and to be responsive to their needs. Being charismatic means learning how to sustain our own good feelings and take pleasure in sharing them with others. And it means noticing, caring, and touching others' hearts in our own unique way.

PART THREE

BRIGHTENING UP THE OUTER YOU

Chapter Eight

How to Send Messages That Attract Others Instantly

*Our body signals make our charisma,
or lack of it, strikingly obvious.*

Without uttering a word, we broadcast potent messages to others about how we feel and think. This silent, steady stream of communication continues, uninterrupted, whether or not we are aware of it and, sometimes, even in spite of our attempts to stop it. We are all judged subconsciously by other people who attach meaning to these messages which we send out via our facial expressions, body positions, and movements.

THE REVEALING LANGUAGE OF THE BODY

The ways in which we express ourselves physically when we stand, sit, walk, and move are dictated by our culture, upbringing, personality, and moods. This nonverbal communication is, for the most part, regarded as being outside our conscious control and, therefore, is a good barometer of how we feel about situations in which we find ourselves, about other people, and about ourselves. With very few exceptions, our body language patently reveals our innermost feelings.

ELEMENTS OF CHARISMATIC BODY COMMUNICATION

When a charismatic person walks into a room, people know someone special has arrived. You may have seen such individuals and wondered what invisible rays made them seem more important and more interesting than most others.

Think carefully for a moment about *how* these charismatic people enter a room. Do you ever remember being fascinated or excited by an individual who shuffled in with his or her shoulders sagging, head drooping, and eyes nervously darting around or staring blankly at the floor? What is your impression of such a person? — that he or she is insecure, ill at ease, or depressed?

Charismatic individuals convey self-confidence and enthusiasm and show that they are on top of things by walking energetically with a confident step, carrying themselves proudly but not pompously. This means they stand tall with head up and shoulders back; then they relax the muscles. Taut musculature causes stiff movements and gestures which make a person seem uneasy and causes others to become guarded and uncomfortable.

A charismatic face is one that is alert, yet relaxed. It is warm, approachable, and inviting. A charismatic mouth frequently curves up at the sides into a radiant smile felt deep within, exposing the upper row of teeth and crinkling the outer eye area. Charismatic eyes dance and twinkle, giving the person the look of one who is vibrantly alive.

Seldom will you see a charismatic person cover his or her mouth, nose, or other portions of the face, or scratch his or her head, while talking. Eye contact is more frequent and of longer duration than that of less confident people. And he or she usually blinks less, appearing to be a better listener than most.

Most often charismatic individuals are free of annoying or distracting habits and mannerisms. If you have ever tried to talk to someone who was tearing a paper napkin to shreds or twirling rubber bands around his or her fingers, you have experienced the negative effects of this type of behavior. Here are examples of some other charisma-robbers.

Tugging at clothing	Gum chewing
Drumming fingers on a table	Spitting, nose blowing,
Tapping pencils or clicking pens	teeth cleaning, or any
Doodling	other behavior that should
Bending or fingering objects	be taken care of in private.
Fidgeting	(Keep in mind that you are
Jangling keys or change	very much within public
Nervous throat clearing	view even when alone in
Nail biting	your car.)

Profane language and inappropriate jokes are also destructive to charisma as are heavy drinking and, for an increasing number of people, smoking. Pipe smoking, with its accompanying habits of filling, packing, and tapping, can be irritating. In addition, the odor of pipe tobacco is unpleasant to some people. Cigar smoking is particularly rude. It shows a lack of concern for others, most of whom find its heavy, lingering smell to be offensive. People who smoke, be it cigarettes, cigars, or pipes, have a disagreeable odor about their person that is immediately recognizable, especially by non-smokers. Not only do their hair and clothing absorb the unclean odor, but so do their automobiles, offices, and homes. And smoking makes a negative public statement about how people feel about themselves.

MASKS THAT HIDE CHARISMA

Publicly, we wear heavy masks that create protective barriers between ourselves and others. We discipline our faces and bodies into these rigid masks to hide the bare human being beneath. We walk along in our own little worlds, keeping a tight rein on the signals we send out; ignoring others on crowded streets and on buses, ever careful not to intrude on their privacy lest we seem too pushy.

Masks are a product of our culture, its prescribed etiquette, and our own psychological defense network. We have masks which are helpful in defining and maintaining our various roles, such as parent and employee masks. And we have masks for various occasions, like parties and funerals.

We need our public masks in order to be socially accepted and to control our involvement with the large numbers of people we meet every day. The plastic smile we show to someone we sit down next to in a crowded restaurant or who we inadvertently brush against in a crowded elevator is part of this much-needed public mask.

We sometimes let our masks slip before children, servants, and people with whom we are intimate. And we often have difficulty maintaining them when we are especially tired, elated, depressed, or totally involved in something. Look around a busy department store in the midst of a holiday sale, notice the faces of the immediate families at a wedding or funeral, or watch someone engrossed in reading a book and you will see some unmasking. Barriers also fall down during great crises such as a war, fire, or flood, when people band together to help one another. At such times, the need for camaraderie and aid overshadow the need for privacy and "non-personhood."

But all too often our masks provide such safety that we are reluctant to take them off or let them down even when it would be advantageous to do so. And some people are emotionally crippled and in social solitary, forever remaining behind their lonely masks. Just as we sometimes need to mask our real selves and hide our real feelings, we sometimes need to free ourselves, to show who we are, and to end the isolation by reaching out and communicating with other people — human being to human being.

Charismatic people are not afraid to drop their masks when the time seems right, for they know that it is difficult for their charisma to shine through them. They frequently allow real contact with other people and are adept at getting them to reveal themselves and to reap the rewards. When the mask is dropped, the tension created by its maintenance also drops, and charismatic power rises. Masking requires a certain degree of energy sometimes better used to boost one's charisma.

Since strangers cannot become friends until they both stop masking, it is important to know how to break through other people's masks as well as how to shed your own.

HOW TO MAKE FRIENDS OUT OF STRANGERS

The most effective way to break down someone else's barrier is to penetrate it while making it seem completely safe for him or her to be without its protection. This can be done by invading his or her personal space in some way, perhaps with verbal contact, close physical proximity, or prolonged eye contact — while sending strong signals that say, "I am harmless. It is safe for you to let down your mask."

Since most people do not know how to do this and others are understandably hesitant, you will probably have to initiate the first move if any interaction is to occur. Charismatic people usually do.

How can you signal others that you are interested in meeting them, however briefly, or in becoming better acquainted while creating the relaxed, comfortable atmosphere which allows them to venture out from behind their masks?

Just as a written invitation sets the tone for a party, in any encounter, your first words, actions, and attitudes set the stage for what follows. Generally, people will reflect your attitude and actions so it makes good sense to adopt those that you want them to express. If you want the other person to drop his or her mask, drop yours. If you want friendliness, be friendly and assume that he or she will be, too. If you want the other person to like you, bet that he or she will and show that you like him or her. We like people who like us.

The well-known and widely used acronym SOFTEN stands for the following key nonverbal signals that can help you to convey openness, interest, and liking. Mastering the use of these is an important part of developing your charisma.

Smile

A good, sincere smile is probably the most effective and universally understood sign of friendliness. It is a gift of good feelings that you give to other people, for when they see you smile, they experience a similar sensation. This transference of feeling is put to good use by actors who make audiences feel the emotion they portray, and by successful advertisers who use smiling models to make potential customers associate happy emotions with their products.

The act of smiling can actually help you to feel happier because the emotion you express on your face causes your involuntary nervous system to go through corresponding changes usually associated with that emotion. So, smiling on the outside makes you smile on the inside.

If you are timid or self-conscious, you probably hide showing any expression on your face, giving you a blank or tense appearance. People like people who are expressive, so make up your mind to let your emotions show. You'll become happier and more interesting to others.

Open posture

Uncrossed arms and legs uncrossed or crossed toward the other person or slightly apart are open body positions. They tell people that you are approachable and interested in them and what they have to say. Positioning your body so you are facing a person directly also indicates openness.

If when you are tense you give in to the natural inclination to fold up into closed body positions (crossed arms pulled in close to the body and legs crossed away from the other person or pressed together), you will add to your anxiety and at the same time signal to others that you are nervous or disinterested. Turning away from the other person gives the same closed signal. Deliberately maintaining open positions when you feel nervous will actually help you to relax and to send positive messages to others. Just as smiling can make you feel happier, maintaining open postures can make you more receptive.

Keep in mind that there may be reasons for another person's body postures other than those mentioned. Crossed arms may indicate disagreement, show stubbornness, or simply mean that someone is cold. The crossing of legs may be habitual and independent of one's emotions. Watch for clusters or groups of cues that send the same message. And consider the context of the situation, too. Only then can you expect any degree of accuracy in understanding the person. For example, if crossed arms are found in conjunction with tight lips and a blank facial expression, it is likely that the person is not open to contact.

Forward lean

We naturally move toward those we like and away from those whom we dislike. Leaning is a natural way for one to signify liking without being overwhelming. Before conversation, it shows interest and is often an invitation to make verbal contact. During conversation, it tells the other person that you are paying attention and are fully involved in what is being said.

Touch

Touch makes a strong, positive impression on people even if it is as fleeting as the accidental one of a cashier as he or she hands you your change. It can convey sincerity, reassurance, concern, or affection and it promotes good feelings between people. Physical contact makes any encounter more personal and meaningful.

Studies have shown that when we touch someone, he or she is more likely to find us to be warmer and more understanding than if we had not touched. For this reason, it is widely used by salesmen to win over customers and by politicians to get votes.

Although the need to be touched is universal and innate, embarrassment, shyness, and concern over how others will react cause us to hold back our natural instinct to express our feelings for others in a physical way. We are conditioned against it. Sadly, we especially hesitate with old and handicapped individuals — those who probably would benefit most.

When is a touch welcomed? When it is an extension of one's personality and an expression of his or her true feelings. What is natural and comfortable is different for each of us. Some people intuitively know how and when to touch. They need only to give themselves permission to begin doing so. Others must experiment to develop their ability to "read" others and to perfect their timing and technique.

The most common touching of strangers is the handshake. Extend your hand confidently, make eye contact, and smile. Shake firmly, squeezing slightly, either with no pumping or with up to a maximum of two deliberate pumps. This tells other people that you are self-assured and glad to meet them. Limp and overly zealous handshakes make immediate negative impressions.

But don't limit yourself to handshakes. Look for other opportunities to touch — perhaps someone's hand or forearm when you are expressing enthusiasm or concern in a conversation, or lightly squeeze a friend's shoulder in passing. Make it smooth, spontaneous, and brief — if you want to keep it from becoming too personal. Generally, the more lingering the contact, the stronger your nonverbal statement.

If you want to test how your first attempt will be received, try touching something that belongs to the other person — something he or she is wearing, holding, or keeps around, such as a briefcase, purse, watch, or book. People feel special about their possessions. Touching one of them usually elicits a reaction similar to, but less extreme than, the one you'd have gotten by actually touching the person's body.

If you find that people sometimes tense up and/or pull away, consider whether your touch may have been too soon, too strong, too long, or in too private a setting. Intimacy feels safer in crowded situations. Also recognize that there are a few people who are uncomfortable being touched no matter how you do it. Part of being charismatic is being aware of such feelings in others and responding by backing off.

A more personal way of touching is to hug. If you're a bit leery of hugging, try side hugs. They are taken less seriously than full body hugs.

Have you seen the automobile bumper sticker that says, "Have you hugged your child today?" No one ever gets too big or too old to hug or to appreciate one.

When was the last time you hugged your child, good friend, mother or father, or grandmother or grandfather? If you're not holding hands with and hugging beloved friends and family members, you're missing out on a wonderful way of letting them know how much they mean to you and how glad you are to have them in your life. And expressing these feelings to them helps to make you special because so many of us refrain from doing so. Charismatic people freely express their feelings for others in a physical way. So get into the habit of touching. Massage a neck, rub a back, hold a hand, give a hug. Doing so can be a very rewarding experience.

Eye contact

The unmistakable twinkle that dances from the eyes of a happy, self-confident, in-tune-with-the-world person grabs our attention in an instant. We are immediately intrigued and we want more.

When we experience deep emotion — any kind of arousal such as excitement, rage, or strong attraction — our pupils dilate, sending out powerful subliminal messages to others. Also, at such times, our tear ducts increase production, giving our eyes that well-recognized shiny appearance. The eyes of an ill, unhappy, or apathetic person lack this luster. The position of our eyebrows and the amount and type of muscle tension in our lids and around the eyes all contribute to the look.

Observe your eyes in a mirror. Are they sending out clear signals of excitement and joy? If not, try to recall an incident in your life that was more thrilling than any other you've ever experienced — the closest thing to ecstacy that you've ever known. Concentrate on that incident and how you felt at the time. Relive the experience in your memory until you feel the excitement of it welling up in you all over again. Feel this overflow of positive energy radiating from your eyes.

Now smile a big smile, tensing and raising the cheekbone area muscles and crinkling the outer portion of the eyes. Allow the smile to fade almost completely, keeping the facial muscles in the same position. Observe your eyes in the mirror again. Are they sparkling brilliantly? That's the charismatic look. With practice, you will become able to command it at will. And each time you do, you will feel happier as the wonderful emotions associated with your look come flooding back. This is caused by the same feedback mechanism that is at work when standing tall makes you feel more self-confident or uncrossing your arms and legs, more receptive.

In order to reach full potency, the charismatic look needs to be directed properly and for the right length of time. In our culture, one-second, blank-faced glances are reserved for things and people who don't interest us much. Our eyes unemotionally sweep over them and drift off apathetically or light on them momentarily, then bounce away. Such looks almost discount others as non-entities. In some situations, they can even connote rejection. Ordinarily, the one-second glances will cause few people to be strongly attracted. A one-second charismatic look, however, says, "Hello. I recognize you as a fellow human being and am glad your path crossed mine." It sends a message of good will that is usually appreciated by others.

The usual two-second look is generally considered to be polite and comfortable to people in most circumstances. It dispassionately says, "I think that you are worth noticing." The two-second charismatic look says, "Not only are you worth noticing, but you are special, and I have singled you out to share in my good feelings."

An ordinary three-second look conveys definite interest. Although sometimes mistaken for staring, it actually pays others an unspoken compliment and issues a silent invitation for them to move closer, to smile, or to speak. But this unfeeling look doesn't provide much assurance that such overtures would be well received. And without some degree of security, many people are reluctant to take such a risk. A three-second charismatic look provides that safety and transmits energy that makes things happen. People react to the strong chemistry, well aware that something exciting is going on. Some feel compelled to make an opening comment; others send signals of receptiveness and wait for the other person to make the next move.

Four seconds or more are considered to be impolite staring. The intensity of this prolonged eye contact is unbearable. Most people automatically look away, although an occasional person may angrily stare back. It is acceptable to stare at objects, but not at people. A four-second charismatic look, too, can easily be uncomfortably strong.

In most conversation, however, maintaining eye contact helps to make a positive impression. The length of time you do so tells others a great deal about you. Depending upon the context of the situation and the accompanying body language, maintaining steady eye contact sends a message:

I am listening with my full attention, and I am
   interested in what you are saying.
I like you.
I am reasonably relaxed and self-confident.
I am sincere and honest.

Avoidance of or minimal eye contact says:
I am bored and thinking about things unrelated to
   what you are saying.
I don't like you.
I feel nervous or self-conscious.
I feel guilty. I am being evasive, hiding something,
   or lying.

Charismatic individuals show their honesty, directness, assuredness, interest, and liking by looking at the person to whom they are speaking as much of the time as is comfortable for them both, only occasionally glancing away to imagine, to recall, to consider, to contemplate, or to ease the intensity of the steady gaze.

When paying compliments or when involved in a positive conversation, charismatic people increase eye contact to its maximum, knowing that doing so accentuates the good feelings.

When the conversation is negative, as it is, for instance, when one person is criticizing the other, a charismatic person reduces eye contact to keep from accentuating the bad feelings.

You can make a better impression than usual even when you feel shy or self-conscious by consciously forcing yourself to establish and maintain eye contact with the person to whom you are speaking. When intermittent breaking of contact becomes necessary and you "don't know what to do with your eyes," try watching the other person's face.

Allowing yourself to continue using eye contact habits typical of shy people only perpetuates the "shy" image. To change this, practice the eye habits of self-confident individuals.

Nod

In conversation, nodding indicates that you are listening and participating. If you don't nod, others may assume that you are disinterested, disagree, or don't understand.

A single nod says, "Yes, I agree."

Smaller, slower nods say, "I understand. Tell me more."

Faster nods say, "I understand. I agree. I want to say something."

Nodding is an important tool of the involved, active listener.

HOW MUCH — HOW SOON?

Chances are that at one time or another you have met someone who immediately seemed very pushy and overbearing or who appeared to want to be chummy too quickly. Perhaps this individual talked loudly close to your face, grabbed your hand or arm, or put his or her hand on your shoulder. Did you feel overwhelmed and try to get away? Being overly assertive or too eager turns people off.

The more you look at, touch, face, and move toward a person, the stronger is the message. The intensity created by using too many of these nonverbal signals at once can easily be too strong, especially the first time you meet someone. And it may hold true for several meetings if the other person tends to be shy, inhibited, withdrawn, stand-offish, or generally distant.

It is important to soften the effect of any one signal by going easy on the others. How can you determine which ones to use and when? Begin by using the least threatening sign first — distancing oneself from another person. Two and one-half to four feet is an appropriate distance at which to begin an initial encounter. If things appear to be going well, you might consider moving in a little closer, but stop one and one-half to two feet away. Closer than this becomes too intimate.

The second least threatening signs are, jointly, facing the other person and using eye contact. If you have moved within two feet of the person to whom you are speaking, it would be wise to turn your body slightly away from him or her and to be somewhat sparing when employing lengthy periods of uninterrupted eye contact.

The third least threatening signal is leaning forward. You can reduce its impact by turning your body slightly away from the other person and/or increasing the distance between you.

The most direct, obvious, and strongest signal is touch. It is a powerful physical intrusion into a person's personal territory. In addition to a handshake, the only acceptable touch in first encounters is probably the "accidental" brush of the hand or arm when handing over items, or of the body when pushed together in a crowded place like a bus, theater, or elevator. Generally, a deliberate touch is well accepted when it is fleeting, especially if it is the result of someone's attempt to express himself or herself more fully. When touching is a natural extension of an individual's personality, it can be more prolonged and can win people over with amazing rapidity.

The first time I was introduced to the world-famous professional golfer Arnold Palmer, I knew immediately he was a pro at meeting people, too. His smooth, gentlemanly manner and engaging smile would have been sufficient for me to have found him charming, but his touch added a special, irresistible quality. Approximately half the time we conversed, he was touching either my hand or arm. He slipped his arm around my waist to pose for a picture, and did not immediately remove it. I was acutely aware of his prolonged physical contact and had observed his similar behavior with others, but I was captivated just the same.

I remember, too, when I first met the renowned mail-order expert E. Joseph Cossman. He held my hand or rested his hand on my arm or shoulder almost the entire time we spoke. It seemed so much a part of his dynamic, outgoing personality that it was completely comfortable and non-threatening.

What works for each person is different. That which works effectively for you may seem artificial or even offensive when exercised by someone else. Develop a style that feels natural to you. Then adjust its intensity to suit the varying personalities, moods, sensitivities, and preferences of those with whom you interrelate. Remember that part of being charismatic is mastering the ability to combine the delicate balance of friendliness and restraint with a goodly amount of responsiveness to the feedback you get from others.

SCINTILLATING SCENTS

Sight and touch are not the only avenues of silent communication. Experiments show that scent traces too small for us to be consciously aware of them can change our respiration, blood pressure, and heart rate. We probably react to people's scent signals as a matter of course without even realizing it.

Many species of insects and vertebrates produce natural substances called pheromones which transmit potent olefactory signals capable of attracting mates, summoning help, or issuing warnings.

Pheromones are scents which all of us exude especially when we are aroused by fear, nervousness, or sexual stimulation. But in our culture, we scrub and deodorize all of them away. Ironically, the same industry that has programmed us to get rid of our own pheromones now routinely adds animal pheromones to certain perfumes and colognes because they have proven to be powerful attractants.

For centuries, people in nearly all societies have used fragrances to increase their magnetism and there is little doubt that it works. But it seems logical that a combination of fragrance and natural human pheromones would probably have the strongest effect on others.

In order to allow some pheromones to come through, it may be preferable to use unscented deodorants. Perfumes, colognes, and after-shave lotions should be used sparingly, especially by men. Many women like the "clean" smell of the male body with just enough of a musky fragrance added to be noticed at close range. Interestingly, the heavy, musky aroma preferred by many women is very similar to the natural substance, androsterone, that is secreted by emotionally aroused men.

Men do not pick up aromatic signals as readily as do women. To get their message across, women should apply sufficient perfume on "pulse" points, such as at the back of the knees, on the neck and wrists, and in the crook of the arm, to be olfactorily noticeable from two to two and one-half feet away. If in doubt about how much to use, chance erring on the side of two little rather than too much, or ask a friend to test at what range he or she can smell the perfume. Overwhelming people with odors of any kind is bound to have an immediate negative effect on them.

Chapter Nine

Mastering Your Use of Messages

*What we feel in our hearts, we
disclose with our bodies.*

Charismatic people each have their own natural style of physical expressiveness which adds life to their words, clarifies their meanings, emphasizes important points, and helps them to make a lasting impression, for we remember what we see far longer than what we hear. And their animated movements hold the interest of others as the human eye is attracted to motion. While the actual postures and gestures may differ from one person to another, they all make a positive statement of self-confidence, openness, conviction, and enthusiasm. We find it easy to believe in such people because their verbal and nonverbal messages complement one another, each verifying the validity of the other.

MIXED MESSAGES AND HOW THEY
SABOTAGE CHARISMA

If you say something and your body says something else, your body will be believed. A frightened face and clutching grip will immediately give someone away even if that person insists that he or she is not afraid. When verbal and nonverbal cues send conflicting messages, the projected image is weakened. However, when a person's nonverbal signals support and supplement the verbal, one's impact is strengthened. When, in addition, the nonverbal actions are expressive, charisma is increased.

Billy Graham has a number of well-rehearsed gestures and postures that add emotional punch to his verbal message. The potent combination of verbal and nonverbal helps to create his aura.

Other evangelists use similarly expressive body language.

For many years, politicians, too, have known the importance of using body language to embellish their words and to elevate their images. Many have succeeded partly because of their ability to project whatever emotion they wanted to with their bodies. What they said often became less important than how they said it. Others have failed because they had not developed this ability. As a result, their body language detracted from, and sometimes belied, what they said. Or they projected an unfriendly, untrustworthy, or awkward image.

You can improve your "eye appeal," add to your overall impact, and increase the believability of what you say by practicing expressive postures and gestures that are consistent with your verbal messages until they become a permanent part of your nonverbal repertoire. This means fully experiencing your true feelings and freeing yourself to translate them into movement. If you are unable to do so, you may not yet have conquered the fear of being yourself.

HOW TO PERFECT YOUR BODY TALK

Most often, people are surprised when observing themselves on video tape. Until they see themselves as others see them, most have no idea what messages their habitual body language conveys.

Chances are, if you aren't getting the response you want, you aren't asking for it properly. Becoming aware of the messages you communicate and which you fail to communicate is the first step to having body language that strongly attracts others.

Popular individuals are keen observers of body signals and know how to use them to interpret other people's unverbalized intentions, implications, and states of mind. In the process of developing this ability, they become more aware of their own body language and are, thereby, more in control of it. You, too, can derive these benefits from becoming a people watcher.

Make it a point to observe the nonverbal language of people at such gathering places as restaurants, parties, and at work. In personal encounters, notice how other people's body signals affect you. When watching television programs, especially those which feature very expressive personalities, turn off the sound for a few minutes. Then turn it back on and check the nonverbal against the verbal messages until you can fairly accurately tell what is going on by observing body talk only.

Think about which postures, gestures, and movements you routinely use. What do they communicate? Which could you delete or change to improve the image you project? Which of those you've observed in others as being beneficial might you add to what you use at present? Practice these until they become automatic.

HOW TO PREVENT THE DAMAGING EFFECTS OF CONFLICTING EMOTIONS

Many individuals unknowingly convey messages opposite of those they wish to. Other people can easily become confused by these false signals. For example, you may consider yourself to be a warm person who wants to make new friends, but if part of you fears meeting people, that reluctance may very well become apparent in your tight, rigid, closed postures and movements that make you seem cold and unaccessible.

If you suspect that you may not be sending clear, honest messages, try to identify what feelings, if any, are preventing you from doing so and carefully think them through. Attempt to resolve the conflict. Consider what message you really want to get across and how you can best do that. Substitute new signals that clearly say what you want for the old, misleading ones. The improvement in the response you get from others may amaze you.

HOW TO BE MORE EXPRESSIVE

If you are shy and refrain from showing your emotions to others, you can teach yourself to be more expressive by practicing gestures, movements, and facial expressions you have found to be effective for others. Exaggerate them. Laugh and have fun with them until you feel reasonably comfortable shedding your old stilted movements for expressive ones. Some people find it helpful to practice in front of a mirror; others find it to be distracting. Experiment to determine what works best for you.

If you have difficulty loosening up, arrange some time to be alone. Turn on some lively music and spend at least ten minutes dancing to it — reaching up high and swooping down low, twisting and turning, swinging your arms, and rolling your head. Really let yourself go. Once you've gotten into the music enough to feel free, try again to execute the new body signals you are attempting to learn.

If your facial expressions are too controlled, close your eyes and tense and relax different series of facial muscles, concentrating on how each feels and on which emotion or emotions it helps to free. Practice expressions that signal various states of mind, such as contentment, happiness, confusion, anticipation, surprise, frustration, excitement, and anxiety. Also try combining expressions; for instance, surprise and excitement or happiness and anticipation. Exaggerate them and hold each for five seconds. Repeat until you become comfortable using them.

When you are somewhat confident in your ability to use your new body signals effectively, test them out in simple, nonthreatening social situations, perhaps with some close friends, and be aware of their reactions. Then begin using them where it is riskier to do so, such as at a cocktail party at which you know very few people. Soon, being expressive will become a natural part of your behavior.

HOW TO GET "IN SYNC" WITH OTHERS

At some time, you have probably seen a couple deeply involved in a conversation you could not hear; yet, you knew that they were getting along well and that they liked each other. Whether or not you were aware of it, you were observing the body-language dance people do when they are on the same wavelength. One person leans forward and places an elbow on the table. Within approximately ten seconds, the other person leans forward and puts an elbow on the table. A tilt of the head and a clasp of the hands, and soon the other person follows suit.

When people are relaxed and like one another, they subconsciously move together. Sometimes they even breathe at the same time. Both of them doing the same thing creates a harmonious feeling which we refer to as being "in sync." At these times, each person feels especially good about being with the other.

Almost immediately, you can establish good vibrations in any encounter by consciously mirroring the other person's moves. If he or she turns slightly and shifts weight from one leg to another, wait approximately ten seconds, then *you* turn and shift *your* weight. In this way you can follow the other person's lead until he or she spontaneously begins to reflect your moves. This rhythmic connection can be established even before anything is said, increasing the likelihood that you will be well received when you finally make verbal contact.

It is also important to notice the other person's natural tempo — the rate at which he or she moves and speaks. A fast-moving, fast-talking person will have difficulty getting "in sync" with a slow-moving, slow-speaking person. Mirroring will work best when you adjust your speed to that of the other person. But be mindful that consciously contrived tempo changes are short-lived. We automatically snap back to our natural range where we feel most comfortable.

Mirroring helps other people to see you as being like themselves in some way. They feel psychologically safe with others who do what they do. Being in the same situation or participating in the same activity at the same time as another person, such as eating, reading, or riding a bicycle, also promotes a "we" feeling which adds to the harmony between them. People develop a feeling of comfort in such situations, although they are most often unaware of why.

Charismatic people are able to recognize that moment when the flow of good vibrations is interrupted. When one person does or says something that makes the other uncomfortable, there are signs indicating that something is out of kilter; for example, a momentary standstill, an abrupt change of posturing, a quick glance away or slight body movement away, and a break in mirroring.

What can you do to get rid of the awkward feeling of sudden disconnection and to restart the dance? Pause briefly. Slow down and quiet down to give the other person some space. Most likely, he or she will have reversed some of the SOFTEN signs in an attempt to pull away from the discomfort. Mirror this person's new, lower level of openness by reversing your SOFTEN signals to match his or hers. Try to determine the cause of the disconnection. If you suspect that it was something you said, change your approach or change the subject. When the other person seems to be at ease, begin advancing the SOFTEN signals, little by little.

Not only can mirroring help you to create maximum rapport with other people at will, but it also can be used to test how someone is responding to you. Give a signal, such as bending your arm, placing your palm under your chin, or crossing your legs — and watch to see if the other person follows your lead. It may be necessary to do this several times before getting results but that person will probably begin to mirror you if he or she feels good about what's going on between you.

Awareness and responsiveness are the keys to harmony between people.

HOW TO TURN ANXIETY, NERVOUSNESS, AND FEAR INTO A BURST OF CHARISMATIC ENERGY

Actors, musicians, and professional speakers are well aware that the nervousness many of them routinely experience before a performance can serve to make them better, more vital, and more alive on stage. They have developed the knack of turning their anxiety into enthusiasm. So why can't your shyness, embarrassment, and fear in certain situations be made to increase *your* effectiveness instead of detracting from it?

Many different emotional states cause us to be physiologically aroused — our hearts beat faster and adrenalin pumps furiously around in our bodies. We are excited. When this excitement is of a positive nature, we are able to think faster and more clearly and respond better and quicker than at other times. But when the excitement is negative, as when we are afraid or nervous, we think slower and less clearly and are less able to be responsive.

If both emotional states are forms of the same physiological arousal, why does one help us to be exciting while the other creates a negative impression? The answer is that when our arousal is the result of nervousness or any other negative emotion, we fight back our increased energy. We try to hold it down by tightening our muscles and reducing or holding our breath. We may use this vital energy to clench our fists or to tense our necks, shoulders, or throats. Our hands or legs may shake or we may have some other of the varied typical symptoms. Meanwhile, we are robbing ourselves of much-needed oxygen by breathing irregularly or shallowly. Our movements are stilted and our capacity to function is reduced. The energy is frozen and so is charisma, for tension and charisma are most often mutually exclusive.

Conversely, when our arousal is the result of great joy, enthusiasm, or other positive emotion, our muscles are relaxed and our increased energy is directed outwardly, toward other people. We become especially expressive and function optimally.

This energy, free of tension, is produced in abundance by charismatic individuals as a result of their ongoing love affair with life, other people, and themselves. It knows no bounds.

How can you liberate the frozen energy you produce when you feel ill at ease? First, consciously relax any tensed muscles while forcing yourself to breathe slowly, evenly, and deeply through the fear. Tell yourself that you are in control of the energy and can direct it anywhere you wish. Experience it as a positive force that adds to your strength and ability to succeed. And use its power to propel you into the fearful activity. Nothing reduces fear like experiencing it and finding you can handle that which has previously paralyzed your resources. Converting frozen energy into free energy takes practice but is well worth the effort.

HOW TO ELICIT THE HELP OF YOUR SUBCONSCIOUS

A child who is frequently told that he or she is clumsy or poor in math is a good candidate to become clumsy or to not do well in math. Thieves who think of themselves as being thieves, most likely will continue to steal, just as obese people who see themselves as being obese will probably continue to overeat. And those who believe themselves to be failures will keep on failing. Why? Because each person, although often unaware of it, tries to live up to the image he or she has of himself or herself. These self-images are locked away in the subconscious mind which works to give form to the images it stores. This important concept has a direct bearing on your ability to project charisma.

If you see yourself as shy and timid, your subconscious will cause you to move, feel, and behave as does a shy, timid person, making shyness and timidity become your reality. To become truly charismatic, you need to change your image of yourself — to see yourself as a charismatic person. When you do, your subconscious will program you to move, feel, and behave like one.

How can you get your subconscious mind to form this new image of you? By repeatedly exposing it to you functioning as a charismatic person. You can do this in two ways — by vividly imagining it and by actually experiencing it. It is most effective to do both.

Begin by observing the body messages sent by people whom you would most like to meet. Particularly notice how such traits as self-confidence, enthusiasm, friendliness, and interest in others are communicated. And be on the lookout for individuals whom you find to be charismatic — perhaps someone you know, a person you see on television, or a character in a movie. Observe them carefully, noting the stances, movements, gestures, and expressions that you think help to create their magnetism.

To get started reprogramming your subconscious, get into a comfortable position and close your eyes. Now slowly relax your body, one section at a time, as you breathe slowly, deeply, and evenly. When you feel fully relaxed, visualize the most charismatic person you've observed or conjure up a composite of those you've seen. Focus on this person until you feel the power of his or her attraction. Then substitute your face and body for his or hers. In great detail, picture yourself sitting, standing, walking, and greeting other people as would the original charismatic person whom you visualized. See yourself exactly as you would like to be — totally self-assured, in complete control, relaxed, and smiling confidently.

All the while, see and feel yourself being enveloped by a brilliant light that radiates great charismatic power. Feel the surge of power from the light pulsating through your body, more and more. Repeat to yourself, "Day by day, my charismatic power is growing stronger and stronger." Experience your excitement as people eagerly respond to the forceful energy you exude. See them being drawn into your glowing bright light of charismatic power.

Do this mental imagery exercise for five minutes at least once daily. Especially good times are just before falling asleep at night and just before fully awakening in the morning as you slip from one mental state to another. These are the periods when you are most receptive to visualization. It is important to vary the scenes of your mental movies to keep them fresh and interesting and to allow for you to experience your charisma in many kinds of situations. See yourself with different people in different places each time.

The next step toward getting your subconscious to help you to project charisma is simply to act as if you have it, using the same body language signals you have experienced successfully in your visualizations. The key is practice, practice, practice, for just as your personality affects your body language, so your body language affects your personality. When you frequently imitate the postures of a self-confident person, for example, you begin to feel more sure of yourself, which in turn, makes it easier for you to act self-confidently.

At first, you will be acting the part within your own mind and in the real world. Pretty soon, as your new role becomes increasingly comfortable and natural, people will think of you in terms of the part. Ultimately, you will become the part in every sense. In time, the pretense becomes a reality. At this point, you will believe yourself to be charismatic and charismatic body language and feelings will have become automatic as your subconscious gives form to its fully assimilated new image of you.

Chapter Ten

The Sounds of Charisma

*Mastering the use of your voice enables
you to bring out the good in others
and the best in yourself.*

No matter how strongly we attract people, we can easily destroy the image we've worked so diligently to project the moment we open our mouths. For we are judged not only by how we look and behave, but by what we say and, perhaps even more so, by how we say it.

Our voices are as unique as our fingerprints. They can make the most elegantly worded message lose all its beauty or can greatly enhance the most simple statement. And they, more than words, reflect our deepest thoughts and emotions.

Our voices paint vivid personality profiles that affect how people perceive us. They can be important assets or insurmountable liabilities, causing us to be liked or disliked, respected or discounted. They can get us listened to, understood, and sought after, or ignored, misunderstood, and avoided.

A well-used voice is natural, smooth, and clear. It is easy to understand and pleasant to listen to. A charismatic voice is, in addition, expressive and confident. It calls attention to its user and to the content of what he or she is saying rather than to itself.

WHAT IS YOUR VOICE IMAGE?

Do you speak up confidently or do you mumble or speak too quietly or hesitatingly? Is your voice quality appealing to listen to or is it whiny, shrill, breathy, nasal, squeaky, or raspy? Is it monotonous or interestingly varied in tone, speed, and pitch?

Does it add to or detract from your visual appearance?

If you are unsure, how can you tell the way you sound to other people? — by tape recording several of your conversations and analyzing what messages your voice characteristics convey. (It may be easiest when on the telephone although our phone voices differ somewhat from our usual speaking voices.) Is this a voice you enjoy hearing? What does it tell people about you? Does it project the image you want?

We tend to regard our voices as being permanent — a fixed part of us. But vocal characteristics that are not due to our anatomy have been learned by imitating other people, or by accommodating the listening preferences of parents, and are affected by our self-images. Our voices are habits and just like body language or any other habits, they can be changed.

HOW TO DEVELOP YOUR OPTIMAL VOICE

It is helpful to observe others when attempting to improve your voice just as it is when trying to change your body language. Listen carefully to those around you, identifying vocal characteristics that help and those that hinder their images. It may be easiest to concentrate when you are not distracted by seeing the person, as when you are on the telephone or listening to the radio, or have turned off the picture when watching television. Particularly listen to those who gain and retain your full attention when they speak. Notice what qualities make them special. Hear the crisp vowel sounds of the English and the resonant quality of the Italians. Become aware of what comprises great voices.

Pitch, Quality, and Force

Your natural pitch level and breathing pattern produce the best sound with the least amount of effort. Listen to a baby's cry. It has an uninhibited, clear, dynamic sound that can be used at full volume for hours without cracking or causing the soreness, hoarseness, or raspiness experienced by many adults when using their voices for prolonged periods of time. Small children still use this natural voice when crying, whining, or shouting. When often told, "Quiet down. You're too noisy," children do more than just lower their volume. They learn to alter their natural voice production to accommodate their parent's ears. These new, inhibited voices lack the clarity, power, and stimulating vibrations typical of natural voices.

You can rediscover your natural voice by listening to small children and imitating their voice production patterns. Call to a friend down the street as would a child, "Hey, Stanley. Can you come over to my house?" Or shout, "That's not fair!" When you achieve a clean, pure sound, practice using it in your everyday speech.

Rate, Articulation, and Volume

Choose a written story and familiarize yourself with it by reading it aloud. Then read it into a tape recorder. Play it back, analyzing your delivery by asking yourself such questions as: Is my speech easily understandable? Is the meaning clear? Do my speed and pacing permit time for listeners to visualize what I have described? Do I use pauses and variations in loudness for emphasis and to add interest? Is the overall volume comfortable to listen to? Do I sound confident?

Decide what you might do to improve the impact. Practice the desired changes and, once again, read it into a tape recorder. Evaluate your progress. Incorporate what you have learned into your daily conversational speech. Remember, changing habits requires frequent and persistent practice.

Expressiveness

Charismatic individuals have expressive voices that are fascinating to hear even when what they say is not particularly clever or profound. Their voices are a vehicle which they use to share their deep emotional reactions to the world they so fully experience. Free, full expression gives life to their words, emotionally involving others. Their voices send gut-level messages that captivate the imagination, warm the heart, and touch the essence of people's beings.

To be expressive, one must be willing to risk exposing heartfelt emotions to the scrutiny of other people. Those who have a tendency to hold back feelings when they talk, most often are so preoccupied with making a good impression that spontaneity and expressiveness are squelched; yet, ironically, the best impression is made by those who are spontaneous and expressive.

If you are restrained because you're afraid that letting go emotionally will cause you to get carrried away and lose control, to be overwhelming to others, to sound silly, or to lose your train of thought, it is important for you to prove these fears to be unfounded.

The best way to become more comfortable being expressive is to practice being that way. It is helpful to read a brief, emotion-laden story aloud into a tape recorder. Then imagine yourself to be an actor in a play, portraying a strong, self-confident person. Read the story into the tape recorder again, but this time do it as would the character in the play. If you really get into the role, you will notice an increase in feeling in your voice over that of the first reading.

Now try it again, reading the story as you would relate it to friends if it were true. Compare this reading with the first one. Have you become more expressive?

Think of yourself as being expressive and try to act as if you are when talking with people. The more you do so, the more natural it will become. It will feel better and better to share the real you with people, unencumbered by old inhibitions.

Tone

The tone of your voice adds an emotional wallop to everything you say. It indicates your attitude toward what you are saying, toward those to whom you are speaking, and toward yourself. Regardless of one's actual words, many feelings are immediately apparent; for instance, irritation, disillusionment, friendliness, confidence, aliveness, and warmth.

Consider which qualities may be evident in your usual voice. By these you will be judged and people will react to them. When long lasting, these qualities are reflections of corresponding personality traits. You can actually bring about changes in those traits by changing your voice. Using a confident tone makes you feel more confident; a calm tone, more relaxed; a warm tone, more friendly. Changing your voice can be an important tool in improving your personality.

HOW TO INFLUENCE OTHER PEOPLE'S ATTITUDES WITH YOUR VOICE

Your tone of voice can decrease other people's negative emotions and increase their positive ones. There are two facts that make this possible:

People automatically tend to imitate the voices they hear.

Think about it. When you whisper or raise your voice, don't others whisper or raise their voices, too? And don't people easily pick up such characteristics as accents, and talk faster or more slowly depending upon the speech rate of the person with whom they are conversing? Emotional tone is also imitated. An angry voice invites another person's anger. Friendliness solicits friendliness, and warmth begets warmth.

A person's feelings can be affected by the voice he or she uses.

Since people usually experience the emotion their voices express, getting someone to imitate your positive voice can actually change his or her feelings. By choosing the proper tone, you can diffuse hostility, soothe irritation, promote friendliness, pacify dissatisfaction, elevate enthusiasm, and heighten happiness.

Practice listening for the feeling underlying what people say. Then alter your voice to fit their needs. How can you know which tone will work best? You do it by using the one that reflects the attitude you want the other person to adopt.

In one experiment, a group of telephone operators were trained to identify emotions expressed by customers' vocal tones. It was determined that the tone of the operators' answers had a definite effect on customers. Operators responded to irritation with warmth, for example, and found that customers became less upset. And when dull-voiced customers were spoken to energetically, many were enlivened.

This ability to influence people's emotions can be invaluable in a variety of situations. You, too, can develop it by learning and using three basic laws of voice conversion.

> Imitating another person's tone reinforces the quality he or she is conveying.
>
> Matching and elevating another person's tone heightens the quality he or she is conveying.
>
> Using a tone opposite that of the other person reduces or brings out the quality opposite the one he or she is conveying.

Can you remember having been extremely excited about something and having shared it with a friend who also became very excited? Weren't you thrilled to have told him or her and didn't that person's excitement feed your own? And if he or she became even more excited than you, didn't your excitement escalate? But how did you feel if your friend said in a listless, apathetic voice, "Oh, that's nice"? Didn't your elation spiral downward?

You can increase good feelings by responding to a positive vocal tone with a like tone that is more intense. Negative tones can be balanced out by using their positive counterparts. This means, for example, that you do well to answer someone's nervous tone with a calm one. Your low, relaxed voice can tranquilize. But, what is more important, the natural tendency to reflect your tone will reduce the level of nervousness in his or her voice, which, in turn, will help him or her to feel less nervous.

SOUNDS OF THE NEW YOU

When you rid yourself of the stress created by fearing what others think, the beauty of your natural voice will be set free. When you develop it correctly and make it consistent with your desired personality, you will project a positive voice image that will get good feedback from other people, improving your self-image. Increasingly, you will see yourself as a self-assured, exciting person. Once again, imitating the person you wish to become will help to transform you into that person.

Chapter Eleven

Conversational Strategies That Boost Charisma

*What you say and how you say it
reveals your inner life to others.*

Charismatic individuals know that their happiness and success are largely dependent upon their ability to express themselves. They are expert at making contact with others. They seem to effortlessly turn strangers into acquaintances, acquaintances into friends, and friends into intimates. They have mastered the secret of using talk to bring out the best in others and to make them feel good. People immediately warm up to them and choose their company over that of others. They sustain the interest of those they have attracted by making conversation with them enjoyable and stimulating. Their verbal know-how draws people they like into their lives and helps to keep them there. Charismatic people seem to have the "gift of gab," but being able to communicate easily and effectively is a skill they have learned.

If you find that talking to people is difficult, you are far from alone. We interact daily with a multitude of them. Each encounter provides an opportunity to enrich ourselves and others — a chance most of us miss. Why? Because as children we are taught how to form words and to make sentences, but are not trained to use them to communicate advantageously with others. For most of us, becoming a good communicator is a sometimes frustrating, lifelong trial-and-error procedure. But good verbal skills can be learned easier and faster. Anyone can learn to use language as a tool to enhance his or her image and to enrich the experience of being with people.

HOW TO FEEL CONFIDENT TALKING TO PEOPLE

As we know, a feeling of confidence is necessary in order to project charisma. Being confident means being sure of yourself — firmly believing that you are worthwhile and likeable and that you have the ability to carry on an interesting conversation. Your confidence in talking to people will increase if you:

Accept yourself and be yourself.

Fully accept who you are and always be that person. Those who are able to express their inner lives to others are happier individuals than those who cannot. And they are more interesting for they share the many facets of themselves that make them unique. Their private thoughts and feelings intrigue us. And we are greatly affected by the enthusiasm and excitement they have when talking about the things they feel most passionately.

Individuals who have not fully accepted themselves are reluctant to share these things. Fearful that others will not accept them, they apprehensively refrain from being themselves, causing them to feel alone even when in a crowd or when talking to a friend. Many have a gnawing concern that their opinions may be thought to be wrong, their interests appear dull, their experiences prove boring, and their dreams seem silly — often the opinion they have of themselves. This hesitancy to show themselves as they are short-circuits their charismatic energy.

Develop yourself and be well informed.

The stress that results from thinking you have "nothing to say" can be alleviated by developing a large repertoire of subjects you can talk about. Stretch yourself to learn and to do new things. See new places. Explore your curiosities and interests and develop dormant talents. Keep up with new trends and developments by reading the newspaper and magazines, including those on subjects unrelated to your usual areas of concern. Gather knowledge on at least one subject until you become expert at it. Feed your mind regularly by taking lessons, attending lectures, listening to cassette tapes, reading books, going to movies and plays, and by exposing yourself to a variety of people who do and like different kinds of things.

Making the most of yourself will increase your self-esteem and will help you to see yourself as a person who has merit. As a mentally, emotionally, and spiritually enriched person, you will radiate the completeness typical of a fulfilled person.

Become a student of human nature.

Learn the basic principles of human behavior. The more you know about people's needs, motivations, and probable reactions, the more sure you will be of your ability to deal effectively with them.

Have good command of the language.

Two people can relate the same story. One account can be fascinating and the other, boring. What makes the difference? The way in which the story is told. Your phrasing and the descriptiveness of your words can greatly increase people's interest in what you have to say and their understanding of what you mean. And an educated usage of language has a definite advantageous effect on the image you project.

Do your homework.

Whenever possible, learn something about people you expect to meet ahead of time, perhaps by asking someone who knows them. Become informed about at least one subject each person could relate to.

If you are to meet a public personality, read up on who that person is and for what he or she is known. Use that information in conversation.

When seeing a person a second time, plan for the encounter by recalling from your past conversation areas of concern and topics that particularly interested him or her. Ask about and expand upon these subjects.

Focus your attention on getting to know more about the other person.

In my charisma classes, I ask students what they were thinking about when conversing with fellow classmates for the first time. Those who experience the most stress nearly always say they were preoccupied with what kind of an impression they were making. They report having such thoughts as, "Do I look good enough?" "Does he or she like me?" and "What am I going to say next?" Their minds were also cluttered by measuring themselves against those with whom they spoke. "Are we equals, or is he or she inferior or superior to me?" And many such students admitted to feeling competitive and judgmental during the conversations.

The most stressful and, consequently, the dullest conversations are those in which these kinds of thoughts divert both participants' attention away from where it needs to be — on what is being said and on getting to know more about one another.

Realize that no one is 100 percent confident.

People intimidate themselves and increase their nervousness by assuming that others are more confident than they are. Usually they aren't. When talking to people for the first time, realize that they are probably at least somewhat tense and are likely to be concerned about the impression they are making on you. Concentrating on relieving their discomfort directs your attention away from yourself, making you feel more at ease and in control of the situation — prerequisites to feeling confident.

SOME BASIC DO'S AND DON'TS OF CHARISMATIC CONVERSATION

Do:

1. Talk positively and be uplifting.

People identify the messenger with the message itself. Think for a moment of your feelings about someone who habitually dwells on the down side of life — one who loves to relate the latest bulletin on crises, shortages, and crime. With this type of individual, "How are you?" prompts a continuous stream of information about his or her current physical ailments, setbacks, defeats, failures, and other problems. The message is that life is bad, painful, cruel, unfair, and depressing. We come to associate this person with gloom, doom, and other bad news that totally obliterates any chance he or she may otherwise have of being charismatic. Instead, people are turned off and driven away.

Stop talking about impending personal and public disasters, emptiness, and fear. Concentrate on present opportunities, joys, and blessings. Talk about today's successes and tomorrow's dreams. Talk of beauty, possibilities, and fulfillments. Speak words that build hope, faith, encouragement, confidence, and those that help people to laugh and to have fun.

Time spent with you will be elevating — a gift of happiness, joyfully shared.

2. Recognize and speak of other people's specialness.

Speak words that help others to discover and to experience their gifts, talents, and special abilities. Make them feel valuable and appreciated.

3. Talk with respect, showing you believe them and their ideas to be worthy of your attention.

4. Show genuine interest in people and what they have to say.

5. Try to find something to like in everyone.

6. Be open-minded and tolerant of attitudes and opinions different from your own. Try to understand other people's perspectives by entering their frames of reference.

7. Be able to say "I'm sorry" or "I don't know" when appropriate.

8. Protect other people's egos.

9. Get people's names correctly and make an effort to remember and to use them.

10. Try to relax and to be spontaneous.

Don't:

1. Gossip.

2. Name-drop.

3. Talk about your possessions.

4. Interrupt.

5. Relate insignificant details.

6. Monopolize the conversation with lectures or long stories.

7. Debate points that come up in conversation.

8. Relate everything to yourself.

9. Try to impress by being clever or witty.

10. Kid, tease, or be sarcastic.

11. Put people on the spot by asking potentially embarrassing questions or those to which they probably won't know the answer.

12. Put people down, even indirectly.

13. Be evasive about yourself.

14. Look for flaws in others.

15. Force your views on people by telling them what to do, how to live, or what they should feel.

HOW TO BREAK THE ICE

Charismatic individuals seem to effortlessly start conversations with new people everywhere — in libraries, gasoline stations, drug stores, and at parties. But their success in approaching people results from their continuing efforts to employ the planning process they have learned so thoroughly — choosing receptive people, assessing the chances of success in the existing situation, deciding upon an approach strategy, rehearsing mentally and delivering the opening lines. They become so adept at it after many real-life attempts that they automatically go through the steps, often barely aware of doing so. They develop an instinct for what will work that tips the odds of succeeding in their favor. You can learn to do the same.

Who is likely to be receptive and under what circumstances?

Individuals considered to be good risks are

alone or with one other person (not conversing at moment of your approach),

in a non-threatening situation (populated surroundings and daylight hours thought to be safest),

experiencing what you're experiencing or doing what you're doing (eating, jogging, riding an elevator or airplane, washing clothes in laundromat, attending a play, movie, concert, or ball game, or waiting anywhere), and

giving it's okay-to-make-verbal-contact signals (open body language, inviting facial expression, looks and smiles directed to you, and responsiveness to your initial body-language signals).

Members of the opposite sex who are attracted to you may show additional signs of interest, such as

giving a sweeping gaze past you more than once, crossing your line of vision, or catching your image while appearing to be looking elsewhere,

allowing you to catch him or her looking at you lingeringly, often drifting into a shy glance downward, assuming various stances and postures that accentuate one's masculinity or femininity such as pulling in stomachs and puffing out chests,

displaying an upper teeth or upper-and-lower-teeth smile,

employing a head toss, head tilt, shoulder roll, or shrug,

making a move nearer to you,

turning up and openly exposing the palms of the hands,

using exaggerated motions,

touching his or her body or stroking an object,

adjusting clothing, and

yawning, twitching or displaying other movements sometimes indicative of conflict or nervousness.

Individuals considered to be poor risks are

part of a group of three or more,

in threatening situations (for example, alone in a parking lot, especially at night),

occupied (deeply engrossed in conversation, a task, reading material, or obviously hurried), and

giving leave-me-alone signals (closed body language, blank, angry, or preoccupied facial expression, tight lips, narrow eyes, cold-shoulder response to your initial nonverbal signals).

What to say.

Once you've made up your mind whom to meet, you'll need to decide what to say. Your initial goal is to interest the other person and to involve him or her in conversation. Once two new people have spoken to one another, however briefly or superficially, further conversation becomes easier. Even asking someone at a gathering, "Where is the bathroom?" will make it more comfortable for that person to say something to you later. Once the verbal barrier is broken, the feeling that the other person is a stranger diminishes.

Contrary to popular belief, research has shown that it makes little difference what you say. What is important is to establish verbal contact. Clever, witty, or profound opening lines are not necessary. Almost any ordinary comment will suffice except those that are negative ("Crummy day, isn't it?"), too direct ("You look like someone I could really hit it off with. Let's go get a cup of coffee."), cute ("Odds are that you're a Virgo because my own personal survey has shown that 99% of all blond, left-handed women with freckles are Virgos."), or over-used, ("Do you come in here often?"). Such openers are usually not well received.

Stating a fact ("This is the third golf tournament to be held here this year.") is not the most effective type of opener because it may or may not be of interest to the other person and it does not encourage a response. But it does have a definite advantage in that it invites a person to talk without obligating him or her to do so. A reply shows a willingness to engage in conversation.

Expressing an opinion ("I really like this restaurant. It has the best clam chowder I've ever tasted.") is usually more effective than stating a fact, but it is not as stimulating to conversation as is asking a question. Because it requires an answer, a question pulls the other person into conversation.

Whether you state a fact, voice an opinion, or ask a question, you'll need to choose a topic. You can make a comment about yourself, but most people won't be interested and rarely will they become involved. You can comment on the other person, but it may seem too personal if addressed to a stranger. A very safe and quite effective topic is the situation or something in the environment in which you both find yourselves.

Depending upon the context of the situation, you may choose from the following topics listed in order of decreasing safety.

MOST SAFE
(True motive
of wanting
to relate
socially is
camouflaged.)

Pretext. Approaching someone with a pretext means having an excuse for making verbal contact. It usually involves asking a question to obtain seemingly necessary information, sometimes concerning a common activity or task.

"How do you operate this duplicating machine?"
"How often does the bus come by this stop?"
"I'm new in this department. Can you fill me in on the background of this memo?"

Situation. Any situation which you share with another person provides you with a topic that is of interest to you both.

To a fellow student you might say:
"What do you know about this professor?"
"When is the next exam?"

To a fellow club-meeting attendee:
"What made you decide to join this club?"
"Tell me, what kind of activities does this club sponsor?"

To a fellow employee:
"What's that new project you're working on?"

To a person standing in line near you:
"What have you heard about this movie?"
"Am I imagining it or is this line moving faster than usual?"

To a customer in a drugstore:
"Why do you suppose it's so crowded in here today?"

Shared focus. Whatever you are both experiencing (seeing, hearing, smelling, or feeling) in your shared environment is a good opening topic.

In a bakery:
"Um, smells like croissants."

In a bar:
"The music's good in here, isn't it?"

In a bookstore:
"That's a wonderful book you're looking at."

Observation about the other person. Observe what the other person is wearing, holding, doing, or saying, and comment on it or ask for more information about it. This works especially well because we all like to be noticed.

"That looks like a SureFlight tennis racquet. Would you mind telling me how you like it? I've been thinking of buying one."
"You're an excellent bowler. How did you get so good?"
"The suggestion you made at the staff meeting was well thought out. How did you ever think of it? Can you tell me more about how it works?"

LEAST SAFE
(True motive
of wanting to
relate socially
is obvious.)

Semi-direct interest. Directly conveying your interest in the other person may sometimes be viewed as flattering and other times as offensive or threatening. Holding back one's true motives at first and tearing down social barriers slowly usually helps to create the emotionally safe, low-anxiety atmosphere most conducive to relating. Carefully weigh the likelihood of success before deciding to employ a direct approach.

"I saw you sitting here and couldn't resist coming over to say 'hello.' "
"I'd like to get to know you. Do you mind if I join you?"

Whenever initiating a conversation with someone new, remember to:

Make sure you don't appear too confident. Doing so may intimidate the other person and cause him or her to feel either overpowered or compelled to maintain the same high level of assertiveness. Talking to you then becomes work.

Be alert. Paying polite attention is not enough.

Be friendly and sound casual. Serious formality stifles conversation. Being too intent upon getting a favorable reaction exaggerates a rejection into life-and-death proportions and puts unnecessary pressure on the other person.

Take your time. After making your first comment, wait for the other person to make eye contact, indicating that you have his or her attention, before going on with whatever you have planned to say. Take time to evaluate nonverbal messages and to respond appropriately to the other person's reply.

HOW TO MAKE SMALL TALK

Most of our talk is small talk. We use it with strangers to be courteous and hospitable and with friends to provide a warm-up period before launching conversation into more meaningful subjects. With new acquaintances, small talk is an audition for friendship. It sends out feelers that seek subjects of common interest. Small talk can establish connections that form the original basis of a friendship or it can convince us not to pursue one.

Some people have a small-talk style. There are interrogators, anecdote-tellers, gossipers, and sermonizers. However, the ideal small talker balances out speaking and listening, revealing little parts of himself or herself and drawing out the other person. This person is more concerned with being interest*ed* than in being interest*ing.* Rather than just nervously filling silences, skilled small talkers use superficial topics as data collectors to determine whether there is enough likeness to make a relationship with someone new worthwhile.

Small talk isn't meant to be brilliant. Overall, we make too big a deal about it. It begins with greeting rituals and cliches such as, "Hi, how are you doing?" "What's new?" "What do you think of this weather?" and proceeds to the second level of communication — an exchange of facts.

These facts can be about something in one's immediate environment, public personalities or events, individuals one knows personally, or the basic facts of one's life. For example, "These grounds sure are well manicured," or "I go jogging three mornings a week."

Briefly discussing such topics provides time to get a "feel" for each other and to establish comfort in relating, but if the conversation gets stuck at this level, charisma is jeopardized. Each person will walk off, never really having met the exciting, charismatic person within the other. The sharing of each person's unique combination of knowledge, experiences, and feelings is what makes conversation stimulating and memorable. Each person becomes real to the other — special and set apart from other people. It is opinions and preferences that make conversation and people interesting.

HOW TO MAKE MEANINGFUL CONVERSATION

You can begin to find out who the other person really is by asking what he or she thinks of something. At this beginning level of meaningful communication, you may want to choose "safe" subjects of current interest — perhaps a particular movie, play, or book. If that person hasn't seen or read it, he or she will probably either ask you about it or discuss one that has been seen or read. Other good topics are sports (mention a winning team and see what happens) and food (may bring out the other person's interest as a gourmet or vegetarian, his or her struggle with a diet, or lead to discussion of health or exercise).

Most everyone seems to dislike the dull, non-productive, preliminary verbal exchanges of name, rank, and serial number — "What's your name?" "What do you do?" and "Where do you live?" Often, people resent being pigeonholed by their occupation, and some who dislike their work feel negative when asked about it. You can instantly convert an exchange of such facts to one of opinions and preferences by expanding upon and redirecting questions asked of you. For example:

QUESTION: "What do you do?"

SIMPLE   "I do emergency road repairs on automobiles." (Requires that another question be asked to keep the conversation going.)

EXPANDED   "I do emergency road repairs for the California Auto Club. I start cars that have dead batteries, take gasoline to those who run out, and do towing." (Factual and impersonal. The other person wants to know about you — not the details of your job.)

EXPANDED AND REDIRECTED   "I do emergency road repairs for the California Auto Club and the most fascinating part of it is seeing the various people's reactions to being stuck. I'm getting pretty good at calming down the ones who're upset." (Tells something about the interests, attitude, and behavior of the speaker.)

Telling what is difficult, interesting, or how you feel about almost any topic will make the conversation better than will the telling of facts. If your conversational partner answers your questions with simple or expanded replies, ask what he or she finds to be the most perplexing, challenging, or rewarding. Doing so will lead that person into a redirected answer.

In the best conversations, both people disclose themselves at about the same rate. You can encourage the other person to open up by first revealing something about yourself. Most people will model their degree of openness after yours. When both participants begin to unveil their real selves, small talk begins to move into the realm of meaningful conversation.

The deepest, most meaningful communication is that which expresses feelings. At this level, conversation becomes a sharing of one's inner emotional life.

The amount and intensity of one's disclosures should be consistent with how well the two people involved know and care about each other. Baring one's most treacherous conflicts, upsetting weaknesses, and heartfelt emotions to a new acquaintance will drive him or her away, while the expression of less intense feelings can help to bind that person to you. The sharing of feelings cements friendships and creates real intimacy. Unfortunately, shy people commonly fail to express any feelings, often stunting the growth of their relationships.

HOW TO KEEP THE CONVERSATION GOING

A major concern of many people is that once past the initial remarks, they will be unable to think of anything to say. The ability to maintain a free-flowing conversation is dependent upon one's ability to introduce various topics related to the existing conversation, and to use verbal techniques that promote conversation.

Verbal techniques that promote conversation and convey interest.

Using conversation facilitators.

A conversation facilitator is a word or short phrase that conveys interest, reflects what has been said, and encourages the other person to continue talking.

"Uh-huh."   "That's terrific!"
"Did you really?"   "You must have had a great time."

Asking open-ended questions.

Questions can effectively promote conversation but unless the right kind are posed, the exchange can quickly resemble a police interrogation with one person doing the grilling while the other grunts a series of one- or two-word replies. This scenerio is caused by asking exclusively closed-ended questions — those that begin with "who, when, where, which, are, do," and sometimes "what." They elicit specific facts but lead to dull dialogue and awkward silences unless alternated with or followed by open-ended questions — those that begin with "how, why, in what way, tell me about," and sometimes "what." Open-ended questions encourage the other person to answer at greater length. It is important to keep open-ended questions fairly specific. If too broad in scope ("What's new?"), you'll probably get a stock answer ("Not much.").

By carefully choosing your questions, you can direct the conversation into any desired aspect of the main theme. An individual who has said he or she recently travelled to Italy could be asked about the hotels, food, transportation, people's attitudes, use and availability of products, or any one of dozens of related topics. It would be even better to ask about his or her favorite part of the trip or about the most exciting or unexpected thing that happened there.

Relating similar experiences.

Describing an experience that closely resembles that of the other person validates his or her experience and links you to each other emotionally. Recognition that you have shared a common experience helps you to identify with one another in such a way that further conversation is easier.

Making use of other people's free information.

Free information is unsolicited data given in any conversation. Commenting on the other person's free information or asking about it will provide numerous topics for interesting conversation. Free information includes not only what is said, but what one can see — distinctive clothing, physical features, behaviors, etc.

A. "You certainly have a way with children."
B. "Thanks. I guess it stems from my *college training in education back in N.Y.U.*"

Person A can now ask about B's college days, how he or she decided to enter the field of education, what it was like living in New York, or anything else this free information brings to mind.

Giving free information about yourself.

Provide information about yourself beyond that which is requested or expected. This gives the other person an opportunity to get to know you and to introduce topics of mutual interest.

Listening actively for content and feeling.

Active listening requires one to concentrate on what the other person is feeling and/or trying to convey, and to feed it back to him or her for confirmation or clarification.

Active listening enables you to verify your understanding of the speaker's message while encouraging further conversation. It gets you involved in what the speaker is saying and feeling, taking your mind off yourself and making it easier to think of things to say. When someone confides in you, active listening helps you to show acceptance and understanding of the other person's feelings without judging their validity or giving unrequested advice or empty reassurances. There is healing power in listening without attempting to cure their ills.

Use active listening whenever you are unsure of the other person's meaning or when a message seems unusually important or emotional.

"I won't be seeing you next weekend."

"You're upset with me, right?" (active listening)

"Not at all. I'm going to Arizona to visit my parents."

Or, here is another example.

"There have been a lot of lay-offs at the plant this month and the work in my department is unusually light."

"Sounds like you're concerned about losing your job." (active listening)

KEYS TO MAKING CONVERSATION INTERESTING

Use concrete, familiar words.

Employ words that are common in everyday speech, are easily understood, and are clear in their meaning.

Be specific.

Use names, dates, and places

GOOD   "I was a captain in the 33rd infantry division stationed in Georgia in the summer of '46."

POOR   "I was in the army in '46."

Paint word pictures.

GOOD   "I was covered with goose bumps. My lips were blue and my hands were so cold they hurt."

POOR   "I was very cold."

Say "I" when expressing your opinions and feelings.

Say "I think" or "I feel" instead of "Some people" or "They" think or feel.

Vary your information-gathering techniques.

Use both opinions and facts, sometimes followed by a question.
"I think the new clubhouse floor is beautiful. How do you think it will hold up with all the foot traffic we have in there?"

Use the other person's name in conversation.

We all like to hear our own names. It draws our attention and makes the conversation personal.

Be real.

Mentioning a problem you encountered or a difficulty you faced on your way to achieving a success will make you believable and easy to identify with.

Talk about that which you know and are interested in.
and
Ask about that which you do not know and may be interested in.

People particularly enjoy talking about their hobbies and favorite forms of recreation, their children, their trips, and sometimes their work. How they got started in business or in their careers, or how they met their spouses or boyfriends or girlfriends are also good topics.

HOW TO CLOSE A CONVERSATION NICELY

Charismatic conversation closings give other people lingering good feelings about having talked to you. At the very least, they prevent them from thinking that you are bored with them or with their conversation or that you do not like them.

When saying goodbye to friends, tell them if you are particularly glad to have run into them, have missed talking to them, or have had them on your mind a great deal lately. If their smile, laugh, or the sound of their voice has brightened your day, share the pleasure by saying so. If you are delighted to have met someone you consider a potential new friend, don't be reticent to tell that person how much you have enjoyed the conversation.

Breaking away from someone you no longer want to talk to without seeming impolite or ill at ease requires special care. Improperly executed, get-aways can be cruel and can instantly destroy your positive image. Begin by complimenting the other person about an attribute or something that he or she has said. Then honestly and straightforwardly make a final statement that obviously expresses your intent to end the conversation.

> "It was very interesting to hear about the new ski resort you discovered, Elizabeth. I may try to get up there this winter. I'm going to move on now. Maybe I'll see you later."

If you are unable to think of anything that you can truthfully praise, use a general complimentary statement.

> "Well, I'm glad we had this chance to talk, Terry. I'm going to circulate a bit now and meet some other people."

> "I really enjoyed seeing you again. You'll have to excuse me now. I think I'd better be going."

PRAISE — A TOOL THAT BUILDS CHARISMA

There is a pervasive philosophy in our society that is best characterized by the axiom, "If another woman ever compliments you on your dress, throw it away." Implied, of course, is the concept that we only compliment people about that which doesn't threaten us. We refrain from commenting when someone else looks good, behaves well, or succeeds because of our envy and the fear that we pale by comparison.

But not everyone behaves in this fashion. Charismatic individuals and others with a high level of self-esteem and a strong sense of inner emotional security enjoy praising others without ever feeling that they are downgrading themselves. They expertly use praise as a tool to build positive images.

Praising people about their appearances, behaviors, possessions, and accomplishments, or about what they say or believe in helps to satisfy the deep need we all have to feel appreciated. And it creates a warm, supportive, nurturing environment in which those around you can safely learn, grow, and change. Studies show that complimenting others also makes them more likely to see you as being understanding, caring, and attractive, and encourages them to open up, deepening and enriching the relationship between you.

And praise can get other people to act as you want them to, for it has a definite effect on human behavior. If you're not getting enough of the behavior you want from people, you are likely ignoring or punishing it when you do get it. Why is this true? Because a basic psychological principle states:

Rewarded behavior increases.
Ignored behavior decreases.

It seems that our natural inclination is to ignore behavior we like and to punish behavior we don't like. Charismatic people know this is unwise. It is best to get into a habit of complimenting behavior you want and ignoring behavior you don't want if you desire that others treat you the way you want to be treated.

How to pay a compliment that will be believed.

Never pay a compliment to get on someone's "good side" before making a request of him or her.

Never pay a "you, too" compliment. Returning the same compliment that is paid to you seems insincere.

Don't lavish compliments on people indiscriminately. Be selective. They will have more meaning if not given too freely.

Praise only that which you sincerely like and don't exaggerate. False praise (flattery) does not win people over. More often, it is resented.

Make the compliment personal. Use details that prevent it from applying to just anyone.
GOOD   "You did the best cha-cha of anyone on the dance floor."
POOR   "You're a good dancer."

How to make compliments easy for other people to accept.

Praise a person's behavior or attributes. Compliment what someone does, says, or has, rather than what he or she is.
GOOD   "The way your hair shines in the sunlight is beautiful."
POOR   "You're very attractive."

Follow the compliment with a question, preferably open-ended.
This makes it easy for the receiver to say a quick thank you for
the compliment and to quickly plunge into answering the question. In the absence of a question, more emphasis is put upon
the receiver's response, and he or she is more likely to have difficulty acknowledging it and picking up the thread of the conversation.

How to accept a compliment paid to you.

Honest compliments are valuable, positive feedback from other
people on your attributes and behavior. Allow yourself to feel good
about and deserving of them. And make it a point to help those
who compliment you to feel gratified for having done so. Never
discount a compliment — ("Oh, you mean this old rag?"). Doing
so tells the giver that his or her opinion is invalid and it projects
an image of a person who feels unworthy of praise.

To respond to a compliment, simply smile, say thank you, and
perhaps briefly comment on the subject of the compliment, tell
how you feel about it, and/or express appreciation that the other
person gave it. Then pick up the conversation where it left off
by answering the question (if one was asked immediately following the compliment) or ask one that will get the conversation going again.

"You have the best backhand of anyone on the tennis team."

"Thanks, Ken. I've spent a lot of time practicing these past few
months and it feels great to have the effort paying off. I've
noticed you working on your serve. How is it coming along?"

HOW TO GET THE PEOPLE YOU WANT INTO YOUR LIFE

Once you have chosen someone to meet, initiated a conversation, and discovered common ground that makes a satisfying friendship seem likely, what can you do to involve this person in your
life? Issue an invitation in such a way that he or she will be likely
to accept it.

"Let's get together sometime" is too vague and sounds insincere.
Don't offer to make plans with someone unless you really want
to, in which case you should extend a specific invitation.

An invitation should suggest an activity (preferably of common
interest) and should specify when and where. It is best to present

it in a casual manner. And the less elaborate, the better. Having a cup of coffee is a much smaller first-time commitment than is going on a whirlwind weekend in Las Vegas. Asking for too much reduces the likelihood of your invitation being accepted.

GOOD   "A group of us is getting together for a spaghetti dinner at my house Friday night. It should be a lot of fun. I'd like you to join us."

GOOD   "I have a couple of tickets for the Dodger game next Tuesday night. Would you like to go with me?"

POOR   "What are you doing Friday night?" (requires the other person to make a decision about committing himself or herself before knowing what the invitation entails).

What to do if your invitation is turned down.

Don't immediately decide, as many people do, that the other person doesn't want to be with you. He or she may dislike the activity you've suggested or may have previous plans for the time of your invitation. Whether or not you are given an explanation, suggest another time and/or activity. If you are told "no" a second time without being given a reason, it may be that the other person does not want to get together. If you suspect that this might be true, don't ask why. You may get an answer that will make you both feel uncomfortable.

At this point, it is usually best to say a few casual parting words such as, "Sorry we couldn't work out getting together. Maybe some other time." Then exit slowly and confidently, feeling good about having done your best and being cognizant of the fact that no one can please everyone.

If you think that the other person did not react negatively to you and may have had some other unverbalized reason for not accepting your invitation, a little persistence may pay big dividends. Contact that person a week or so later and try again. Sometimes persistence wears down resistance.

How to accept and turn down invitations charismatically.

Charismatic individuals accept wanted invitations enthusiastically, making others glad they extended them. And they turn down invitations graciously, helping others to walk away still feeling okay about themselves.

If asked, "What are you doing Saturday night?" by someone

you would like to see, don't answer, "I'm not doing anything." It makes you sound less desirable and commits you to an unknown activity that you might dislike or be unable to do. Instead ask, "What do you have in mind?" If the suggested activity doesn't interest you but the person doing the inviting does, don't hesitate to suggest other activities of the same type. For instance, "I'd like very much to see you Sunday but I don't play tennis. Might we go bicycling or skating instead?" If the other person already has tickets or is in some other way committed to the activity, suggest another day and something else to do.

If the same invitation is issued by someone whom you don't want to see again, don't try to get out of it by using some dull activity like cleaning out your sock drawer or washing your hair as an excuse not to go. You'll end up insulting the person by admitting that you'd rather do that than to be with him or her.

You needn't qualify, rationalize, or give excuses for your decision not to accept someone's invitation. It is best to make as honest a reply as you possibly can without hurting the other person's feelings.

"Thank you for asking. Sorry, but I can't make it."

"The party sounds like fun and it's nice of you to invite me but I can't make any plans right now."

It is helpful to follow up your reply with a comment or question about something other than the invitation. Doing so makes it easy for the other person to avoid having to comment on the turn-down and discourages him or her from issuing an alternate invitation. It clearly says, "Let's stay away from talking about getting together." This is the kind thing to do. The unkind thing is to say that you'd like to go but are busy, thereby encouraging the person to continue issuing invitations, dooming him or her to a series of rejections instead of only one.

When declining an invitation, prefacing the refusal with a compliment or two cushions the rejection. Praise whatever you honestly are able to relating to the invitation. When you would like to accept an invitation but are busy, you might reply:

"You're such a great bridge player and I always enjoy the game when we're partners. I'm sorry I can't make it Friday but I'll look forward to the next time you ask me to play."

When you would not like to accept, you might reply:

> "How kind of you to ask. I can't play on Friday but thank you so much for thinking of me."

Blatent honesty can be brutal. Sometimes telling a white lie may seem like the only alternative, but try to be both kind and honest whenever possible.

How to refuse to give out your telephone number without offending anyone.

I am frequently asked in charisma classes how a person can refuse to give out his or her telephone number without being rude. Some students have reported intentionally giving out wrong numbers because they did not know what to say when they were not attracted to the person asking. Others have given out their numbers under duress only to reject the person when he or she telephoned. Both strategies are hurtful.

I have found an effective tactic is to say, "It's very nice of you to ask but I usually prefer not to give it out." If you wish to soften the turn-down, you might add, "May I have yours instead?" This implies enough interest to protect the person's sensitive ego without lying or making excuses. Some people still prefer to tell a face-saving lie such as, "Thank you for asking but I'm involved in a steady relationship right now."

Developing conversational skills takes practice. That means getting out there and talking to people, using what you have learned. Give yourself credit for each little bit of progress, knowing that you are giving yourself a gift you will have for the rest of your life — the gift of gab.

Chapter Twelve

How to Project a Compelling Image (Even If You Think You're Unattractive)

Physical attractiveness is a marriage of what you get from nature, what you bring out, and what you put on.

Our appearance is an advertisement to the world. It tells others who we are and what we want. It conveys specific information people use to determine an interest or lack of interest in us. Like it or not, when meeting new people we are judged by how we look. As they get to know us better, our inner qualities become more apparent and our physical appearance less important.

ATTRACTIVENESS DRAWS PEOPLE TO YOU

An individual may have a great personality and be wonderful to know and exciting to be with but if his or her appearance doesn't attract others, they will never get close enough for long enough to find out how terrific a person he or she really is. Herein lies the first major advantage of an optimal appearance — to attract people to you, giving them the opportunity to recognize and to appreciate your inner qualities.

Must you possess physical beauty to attract people? The answer is absolutely and unequivocally, no. Studies show that we are prejudiced in favor of such individuals, assuming them to be more interesting and intelligent than others. We feel warmer toward them and are more accepting of them, but their beauty is often also a serious detriment. Men who are too handsome lose credibility with other men and "beautiful" people are often lonely. We may admire them from afar but approaching them is risky business. ("Why would big, gorgeous *him* be interested in plain, little *me?*") The fact is that "average-looking" individuals who are skillfully "put together" and appear approachable are far less intimidating and more likely to meet people and to establish new relationships.

Physically beautiful people who are getting by on their looks alone sometimes don't develop themselves in other ways, causing disappointment in them by those who do chance getting close. And as they age, many become uneasy as their one major resource — their good looks — begins to fade away. In the absence of outstanding beauty, most "average-looking" people learn to develop other attributes, thereby often becoming more interesting and socially accomplished than their super-attractive counterparts.

Just as we relate attractiveness to excellence, we relate unattractiveness to a lack of it. So it is of paramount importance to look your best. But remember, that doesn't necessarily mean having classical facial features and a great body. Rather, it means making what you've got count.

LOOKING GOOD MAKES YOU FEEL GOOD

Have you ever noticed that on a "good" day — when your hair immediately falls into place, your skin glows, and, overall, you feel more attractive than usual — you also feel happier and more confident? Don't you stand a little taller and notice others responding to you more readily than they do on other days?

Seeing oneself as being attractive can transform a person's personality. Maxwell Maltz, M.D., author of *Psycho-Cybernetics,* frequently observed this phenomenon in his plastic-surgery patients. Many who had only minor changes made in their physical features experienced major changes in personality, becoming more outgoing and self-confident. A similar reaction to an improved self-image is often shown by subjects of conventional physical make overs. Perhaps you've seen such people on television, both before and after experts have created new hair, face, and clothing looks for them. Haven't you noticed that most of those who had these make overs done radiated an attractiveness they previously lacked that went far deeper than the superficial improvements made in their appearances? When people know they look good, they feel better about themselves and communicate it to others. As we know, feeling good about oneself is central to generating charismatic energy.

I see daily evidence of this principle at work. Just recently, I was consulted by a rather shy, 44-year-old, divorced woman, Marlene, who had left the small town where she had grown up and married to come to Los Angeles one year before. Her appearance was plain and earthy. Her clothing was simple. She wore no make up and had straight, waist-length, light brown hair that detracted from her wide, deep-set, blue eyes. Marlene projected an image of who she used to be rather than who she was becoming.

The first thing we did was to have her hair cut and properly styled to fit her desired image, facial structure, and features. She also had a make up lesson at which she learned how to enhance her best facial features and minimize less desirable ones.

When I spoke to her the next day, a transformation had already begun. She sounded ecstatic as she animatedly said, "My hair looks great and I can't believe how much better I look wearing make up. I feel like a brand new lady."

Someone had even asked her out after meeting her briefly the previous night when she stopped at a girlfriend's apartment to show off her new look. It was the first invitation from a man extended to her since coming to Los Angeles. Although she has a long way to go, she's off to a good start in developing her personal magnetism.

I've observed many people who have experienced the same fascinating thing: They make themselves look better, they feel better about themselves, and others immediately respond better to them.

HOW TO ATTRACT THE "RIGHT" PEOPLE

Increasing your ability to attract people is good for the ego but is not necessarily enough to get the "right" ones into your life. Countless times I have heard the lament, "I always attract the wrong kind of people." Who are the "right" kind? The kind who will like and appreciate you as you are and who value the things in life that you value. If you project an image other than your true one, you will, instead, attract those who want what you're pretending or representing yourself to be. In this case, you will be unable to satisfy their expectations and probably will be unhappy while trying.

To find people with whom you have things in common, you need to use your physical image to advertise who you are and what you want in such a way that the people you want to attract will be likely to respond.

We naturally are drawn to those who are like ourselves. Ivy Leaguers like other Ivy Leaguers. Golfers like golfers. Artistic or academic types like other artistic or academic people. For instance, if you present yourself as a casual type when your true tastes are sophisticated, it may cause you much difficulty.

When you change your image message, often you will get immediate results. Such was the case with Charles, a somewhat reserved, 28-year-old salesman of ladies' apparel. He complained of attracting very outgoing, rather showy individuals whom he was forever trying to please by being lively and gregarious. Instead, he should have been directing his efforts into finding those who liked more moderate, conservative people, like himself.

Because of his job in the clothing industry, Charles thought he had to dress flamboyantly, but as long as he did, the problem persisted. We toned down the colors and style of dress, keeping it current but making it more classic. We restyled his hair to achieve a chic look, and immediately he began to attract people who were right for him. The relief of being able to be oneself and to be liked for it is wonderful.

When evaluating your appearance, consider not only how appealing you appear but how representative your look is of the real you.

THE 4A FORMULA FOR LOOKING YOUR BEST

Achieving one's optimal appearance means skillfully maximizing the raw materials nature has provided to enhance physical attractiveness and projecting an image that honestly reflects one's best inner self. You can achieve your optimal appearance by employing the Charisma Development Program 4A Formula.

*A*wareness
+
*A*ction
+   = Optimal appearance
*A*cceptance
+
*A*ttitude

1. Awareness

It is important to become aware of the overall image you project and of the individual elements that create it. First, take an inventory of your raw materials — those assets and liabilities your genes and life style have provided. Take a long, head-to-toe look at yourself nude, without benefit of hair styling or make up. Try to unemotionally evaluate what you have to work with. Decide whether each of the following is a help or a hindrance in attracting people:

Characteristic	Asset	Liability
	(Check one)	

Hair
  (thickness, coarseness, color)
Complexion
  (color, clarity, dryness or oiliness)
Facial features
  Eyebrows (thickness, shape, color)
  Eyes (color, size, spacing, depth)
  Nose (size, shape)
  Mouth (size, shape)
  Teeth (alignment, condition)
Facial structure
  Chin (protrusion or recession)
  Cheekbones
  Facial shape (round, oval, square, triangular)
Body
  (height, weight, shape/configuration,
  muscle tone, posture, flexibility)

Now stand before a mirror again, this time "put together" as you usually are when beginning a day's activities. Use the worksheet below to record information as you analyze where your current techniques for maximizing your appearance have effectively made the most of your assets and the least of your liabilities, and where they have been inadequate to do the best job possible.

Worksheet
for
Physical Image Projection Analysis

	Very Good	Accept- able	Needs Improvement
Hair			
condition			
color			

     style
Facial enhancements
  glasses
  Men: Hair growth
        (mustache/beard)
  Women: Make up
Complexion
Teeth
  appearance
  condition
Body
  weight
  shape
  condition
Clothing
  style
  color
Grooming
  cleanliness
  neatness
Overall image
Extended image

When evaluating your hair

Look to see if it is clean and in good condition. Is it dull and dry, oily and separating, flat and limp, or shiny and healthy looking? Does the style complement your facial features and shape? Is it current or outdated? Is it appropriate to your age and personality? Does the color enhance your skin tone and eye color? If dyed, is it rich and natural looking? If not, what color might look better? If gray, might it be more flattering another color?

When evaluating your face

Men:

Are you cleanshaven? If you have a mustache and/or beard, does it enhance your facial features or detract from them? Is it trimmed and neat? Does it fit your desired image? If you have neither, might you look more attractive if you did? Does the shape and fullness of your eyebrows complement your face? Are nose- and ear-hair cut?

Women:

Does your make up effectively enhance your best features and downplay your weaker ones? Does it appear natural or call attention to itself? Is it appropriate to your age, desired image, the occasion, and time of day?

If you wear glasses, are they flattering, fit your face and image? Is your skin clear and healthy looking?

When evaluating your clothing

Is the style flattering to your height, weight, and shape? Does it accurately represent your personality or one aspect of it? What statement is it making about you? Is it the one you desire? Is your clothing appropriate to the season, climate, and occasion? Is it up to date? In good taste? Well coordinated? Properly accessorized? Does the color complement your hair, skin, and eye colors? Does it fit properly? Is it in good repair? Is the hem straight and the pants the correct length? Does the fabric texture fit the statement you're trying to make? Do you feel good wearing it?

When evaluating your grooming

Is your hair clean and combed? Nails clean and shaped? Clothing clean, pressed, and in good condition? Are you freshly shaved? Shoes polished? Do you look neat or disheveled? Do you "put yourself together" every day or only when seeing others who "warrant" it?

When evaluating your body

Does your body size and shape enhance or detract from your overall image? Does your posture reflect self-confidence and good health? Are you able to move with ease or do you appear to be out of condition?

When evaluating your overall image

Are all elements of your image making the same unified statement about you or, for example, does your hairstyle say one thing and your clothing another? What is the statement you're making and is it the one you want to make? Do you look like someone you would like to meet?

When evaluating your extended image

Consider your home, office, automobile, and possessions to be extensions of you. Others view them as such. What statements do they make about your values, preferences, and traits? Are they consistent with your body image and personality? What would an individual deduce about you from seeing them? Develop a personal style of clothing, possessions, and personal environments that accurately tell others who you are. These elements help to communicate your individuality — the basis of your charisma.

2. Action

Once you recognize where your strengths are and where you could benefit by improvement, it's time to take action. Don't be discouraged by what nature or your life style has or has not given to you. You can improve on nature. Your clothing, hair style, and, for women, make up are valuable tools capable of helping you to build almost any image you may want. Decide how to capitalize on your physical assets. Accentuate them so the eye is immediately drawn to them rather than to your liabilities.

Liabilities (flaws) can be dealt with in one of the three following ways:

By changing them into assets.

I distinctly remember one of my clients whose worst liability became her most valued asset. When I first saw her she had the bushiest, driest, most strawlike, unevenly colored hair I had ever seen. It was, by far, her most obvious negative feature. We had the color evened out and softened and the hair conditioned and styled. Her soft, shiny hair became her most positive attribute, balancing and framing her strong chin and angular face.

Plastic surgery is sometimes advisable when a flaw is particularly detrimental to an individual's image — either to others or to himself or herself. Often corrected features become the most attractive ones a person has.

By eliminating them

For example, one can get rid of unsightly extra weight by reducing and teeth stains by having a dental cleaning.

By camouflaging them

For instance, the right clothing can help to conceal a multitude of imperfections by giving the illusion of corrected body size and proportions.

Such problems as flaws, scars, and birthmarks can often be hidden by special make up procedures.

Experiment until you find what makes you look best. In choosing clothing, trust your own eye before trusting that of a salesperson. If you need help in planning specific steps to take to improve your physical image, you might ask a close friend whose own image is effectively projected for suggestions. Learn new techniques from current make over articles or books. Or go to a competent consultant.

3. Acceptance

How you feel about your appearance is as important as how you actually look. Some people find it even more important. A survey in which hundreds of males were asked to define "sexy" showed the seven most frequent answers to be self-confidence, composure, intelligence, self-assurance, friendliness, femininity, and being at ease with one's body. Tight muscles and other physical attributes were far down the list. Other studies examining what men and women find most attractive about each other have consistently produced similar results. A flawless body is not necessary to project charisma but a positive attitude about it is.

How do you feel about your appearance? Do you like your face and body? When first evaluating yourself in a mirror, did your eyes gravitate to your problem spots or search out your best attributes? If you look for and dwell upon your flaws, you will likely perpetuate a negative physical self-image that can smother self-confidence and sabotage the image you project to others.

Do you assume that everyone will immediately see what you see and judge you by the one or two negative features by which you judge yourself? This is rarely the case. The truth is that most people are not usually very observant of isolated features and characteristics. Often they don't even notice blemishes and bruises that may have caused us concern. Rather, they get a more overall impression of another's appearance. The imperfections are in the forefront only in the minds of those who possess them.

We get destructively caught up in how we think we should look. Even many of the most beautiful women and handsome men — models, singers, actors, dancers, show girls, and strippers — magnify their imperfections and feel dissatisfied with their bodies. Having a negative body image is the norm. Negative thoughts about our bodies are often indicative of low self-esteem. When this is the case, no amount of physical improvement will alleviate the negative feelings.

One area in which this is particularly true is in that of our body weight. Diet products and books are big business thanks to those who search unrelentlessly for a fast and easy way to get thin. It has become a national preoccupation. One magazine survey of 33,000 people found that 75 percent of them felt too fat; 50 percent were on starvation-level diets or were fasting; 63 percent said their feelings were affected by their weight; 46 percent were self-conscious around almost everyone; one-half of those normal weight or thinner were not satisfied with their weight; and 80 percent of them were still dieting.

The solution is to learn to like yourself as you are, to improve what you can, and to accept that which you can do nothing about — realizing that perfection is unrealistic, unnecessary, and usually based on fluctuating opinions and values of other people, of society, or of the mass media.

What can you do if you actually have a physical problem that is obvious and cannot be changed quickly — if you really are overweight, for example? First, accept yourself as you are — bulges and all. You are much more likely to be able to lose weight and to keep it off if you do not hate yourself for being heavy. That doesn't mean that you're not going to do anything about your weight, but that you like yourself in spite of it. To be effective, improving one's physical self should be a gesture of love for oneself and one's body rather than a result of their rejection. The decision to lose weight should be a conscious choice based on self-love and concern and the desire to look and to feel better. When an individual forces himself or herself to diet because he or she feels unacceptable as is, continuous denial of desirable foods fosters mounting resentment, frustration, and often cheating or binging and, ultimately, failure with a sense of guilt and powerlessness. This entire cycle is incompatible with charisma.

Once you've done all you can about any characteristic you see as being negative about yourself, or you are working on it, direct your mind to developing and feeling good about your best physical attributes. Focusing on your best outer qualities will help you to like yourself better, just as does focusing on your best inner qualities. And the better you like yourself, the easier it will be to change.

But what if there is something about your face or body you dislike that cannot be changed? Physical limitations only become obstacles if you perceive them as such. Jill Kinmont, my quadraplegic roommate at the rehabilitation center, completed college and became a teacher. She also got married. Blind musicians play instruments, write music, and perform professionally all over the world. Such people overcome unchangeable handicaps by accepting what is and by being determined not to let such problems stop them from achieving all they are capable of.

Perhaps you are bothered by a permanent physical characteristic that is less dramataic than paralysis or blindness, but one that you find to be troublesome and limiting — being short, for example. From a visual standpoint, it is helpful to choose clothing colors and styles that give an illusion of height. But the main problem to be dealt with is the emotional component with which many, men especially, often have difficulty. Complaints range from not being taken seriously and being unable to project authority, especially at work, to not being able to find enough short women to date. The answer lies in an attitude change. If short stature makes you feel powerless, so you will be.

A 5-foot–1-inch male acquaintance of mine, named Tony, is married to a statuesque, 5-foot–9-inch model. He runs a business that employs over 75 people who greatly respect him and his obvious business ability. Tony told me that he simply "thinks tall" and gives everything his best effort. He has accepted his shortness and functions optimally by focusing on and developing his strengths.

A major Los Angeles multi-millionaire builder is only 5-feet–3-inches tall. He certainly doesn't think small. Dudley Moore, the actor, is another example of a short man who doesn't limit himself. Apparently undaunted by his height, he established an enviable career in a highly competitive industry and has been known to keep company with women who are considerably taller than he.

Accepting that which cannot be changed is necessary to a healthy self-image. And a healthy self-image is the basis of charisma. Become aware of your appearance for constructive purposes. Do whatever you can to present yourself at your best. Accept and learn to love who you are and how you look. Get away from preoccupation with your body and get into life instead.

4. Attitude

My daughter, Laura, had a little black car that had the right front fender hit by an unknown driver in her high school parking lot. She always paid for her own car expenses and couldn't afford to have the dent repaired right away. Figuring the car looked awful anyway, she seldom bothered to wash it. When she neglected to fix a small tear that developed in the headliner, it grew larger and began to hang down into the car. The automobile didn't run as well as it might have because Laura said the "hunk of junk" wasn't worth having serviced. The more the car fell into disrepair, the more she hated it. The more she hated it, the worse it looked and ran.

Unfortunately, some people do the same thing with their own bodies. Feeling that they are not worth much effort, they get caught up in a self-perpetuating, spiraling cycle of neglect, abuse, and self-hatred. Neglect shows and abuse soon becomes obvious. When our physical selves are not properly cared for, we broadcast negative signals about how we feel about ourselves. The more we like ourselves, the more eager we are to put forth the effort necessary to look as good and to function as well as possible.

The look of the 1980s and the look of charisma are one — healthy, vibrant, well-cared-for faces and bodies that communicate strong messages of self-esteem and positive living. Being charismatic involves not only how one looks, talks, moves, thinks, feels, and behaves, but also how one functions physically. Absence of disease alone is not enough.

WELLNESS IS ATTRACTIVE

When in the state of superhealth, a person has boundless natural energy and appears youthful, agile, and relaxed. His or her skin glows and eyes sparkle with the fresh, radiant look of one who feels great. This fantastic sense of well-being can be attained by living up to one's physical and emotional potential. Physical fitness, nutritional sense, and stress management are the three main routes to a superhealthy, charismatic life style.

Get physical.

I am sometimes told that I am lucky to be thin and to have a nice figure, but luck has little to do with it. I eat reasonably and exercise regularly. As part of my workout, I walk several miles on a treadmill at an aerobic pace at least three days per week.

I, and millions of others, have found aerobic activity to be unique and invaluable in that it not only improves a variety of physical problems, such as those with the back and the respiratory and cardio-vascular systems, but it dramatically increases energy and mood levels while decreasing stress. Psychological research on jogging has consistently shown that it enhances self-esteem, reduces anxiety, and alleviates depression. And numerous artists, writers, musicians, scientists, entertainers, and entrepreneurs claim that aerobic exercise boosts their creativity.

Vigorous, sustained exercise produces a natural high by stimulating the pituitary gland to secrete hormones called endorphins. These morphine-like substances, at comparable dosages, are 200 times more powerful than morphine. Aerobic exercise causes a fivefold increase in the body's endorphin levels, producing an intense, natural euphoria remarkably similar to that which an individual experiences when charisma is at its peak. It's exciting, to say the least. It builds up inside until one can hardly contain it, putting a rosy glow on everything.

The exhilaration can be maximized by thinking happy thoughts while it builds. When on the treadmill, for example, I listen to music on earphones absorbing the beat and flow until they become part of me, while reliving my most exciting recent experiences in detail. Sometimes I visualize myself attaining my most challenging personal goals and fondest dreams. Often it becomes difficult not to laugh aloud, letting the world know how fabulous I feel.

Clinically, the euphoria is expected to last for 30 minutes to two hours after stopping the activity which produced it. However, I have memorized this feeling of pure joy and by focusing on its physical and emotional effects, I can keep it going for many hours and can reproduce it to varying degrees at will, in most circumstances, and without any outside stimulation. If you've ever experienced this feeling of being tuned in and turned on, you've tasted the sheer joy of charisma.

If you do not have a regular exercise routine that includes aerobic activity, plan one. Swimming, walking, and bicycling are three of the most effective, causing the least number of injuries. You might want to choose more than one and alternate them to keep things interesting. Exercising should be pleasurable, so choose activities you enjoy.

Eat smart.

Too many people think that being good to themselves means eating whatever they want in unlimited quantites at any given moment. But just as we discipline our children out of genuine concern for their welfare, so we must learn to discipline ourselves — because we care about ourselves and how we look and feel. Developing sensible dietary habits is an act of self-love, and to be effective we must view it as such rather than as something we are compelled to do out of guilt or dissatisfaction with the way we are.

It is not the ice cream sundae we splurge on once a month or the occasional pizza that affects our health, vitality, and weight adversely; it's the daily consumption of such items in an unthinking manner that causes problems. Eating large, heavy meals and lots of snack-type "junk" foods can make you feel lethargic and gain unwanted weight. Caffeine and sugar can cause wide swings in blood-sugar levels resulting in, among other things, moodiness, irritability, and a low-energy level — all destructive to charisma.

Although the eating regimen that makes each individual feel and function best may vary somewhat, almost everyone does better eating more raw vegetables, fresh fruit, and whole grains than fatty meats, candy bars, and soda pop. In general, a well-balanced diet that is low in fat, sugar, and salt, high in natural foods, and taken in moderate quantities is likely to promote health and vigor.

Learn to relax.

If you're not at peace with yourself, you'll feel ugly and project that ugliness to others no matter how much you work to improve your physical appearance. People appear younger and more attractive when relaxed and happy. Mind and spirit are elements of attractiveness just as the body is. Inner beauty, compelling and long-lasting, is easily overshadowed by tension. Uptight people impress us negatively. Handling stressful situations effectively and calmly is a charismatic quality.

Stress is an undeniable fact of our lives. Who couldn't benefit by having one more hand or a few extra hours in the day? We all experience some negative stress created by trying to cram too many tasks into too little time, by being delayed, or by things going wrong. But we choose to allow such occurrences to upset us, or not. Nervousness is self-induced. We think it into being. What we say to ourselves about what is happening determines whether we become agitated and irrational or remain calm and in control.

Have you ever wondered why some people become tense and irritable and have difficulty coping with their daily pressures while others coolheadedly juggle twice their load? Unstressed individuals evaluate their priorities, plan their time accordingly, and assume the attitude that they are doing all they can and that upsetting themselves about being unable to accomplish more will only serve to slow them down.

Have you noticed how some people stuck in traffic or a long, slow-moving line become annoyed while others do not? Those patient, unstrained individuals seem to enjoy the scenery, converse with people around them, or daydream with pleasant expressions on their faces. They have chosen not to waste one precious moment of their lives by being irritated over things they cannot control. These people don't allow themselves to see every mishap as being catastrophic. And they try to avoid useless worrying.

You, too, can make a conscious decision to have an unhassled attitude. When you feel yourself growing impatient in a traffic jam, for instance, tell yourself that becoming agitated won't get you to your meeting any sooner — only more nervous and less able to make a favorable impression. On a hot, July afternoon, should your car become stalled on a hill, smoke billowing out from beneath the hood and green stuff pouring all over the street, tell yourself that it is not the end of the world — simply an ordinary inconvenience and any amount of irritation you can muster up won't get you on your way any sooner. It will only spoil enjoyment of a forced interlude in your day, perhaps joking with a friendly repair person.

For many years, I was expert at losing my cool in trying situations. Once I realized how futile the bad feelings were and how they added to the unpleasantness, I made an effort to change my reactions. I knew I had succeeded when one night my gold watch slipped, undetected, off my wrist and onto a dance floor, never to be seen again. When I realized it had fallen off, my companion and I searched for it among the dancing couples, but to no avail. He was upset more than I was and repeatedly said I must feel awful and suggested that it might be best for him to take me home. I distinctly remember deciding that although it was too bad that I'd lost my watch, I wasn't going to make things worse by cutting my fun evening short to go home and sulk. We stayed and had a great time once I convinced my friend that "things" aren't worth one bad moment — they can be repaired or replaced but a pleasant evening wasted is gone forever.

The next time you are in such a situation, think about your inner dialogue. Even the worst situations can be improved by keeping them in perspective and having a good attitude.

REAL BEAUTY IS NOT JUST SKIN DEEP

What is most attractive is what goes on inside a person. Inner beauty is an inner harmony and tranquility, a richness of spirit, and a sense of balance in all things. It is comprised of self-awareness, self-respect, self-love, and a sense of fulfillment. It shines brightly, lighting up one's physical self with an unmistakable radiance that makes physical beauties who lack it pale by comparison. True beauty becomes apparent with the development of one's spiritual self.

SPECIAL PEOPLE — SPECIAL ATTRACTIVENESS

Some of the most charismatic individuals are not physically attractive, but they have other critical elements working in their favor. Do you remember the little, gray-haired, grandmotherly woman who starred in the award-winning "Where's the beef?" advertisements, captivating us with the adorable personal quality she possessed? Some time ago, a blind radio interview-show host, Glen Gordon, so enchanted me with his sense of humor, incredible spirit, and sparkling personality that I thought about him for days after having a 20-minute telephone conversation with him.

Powerful attractiveness can be achieved by developing and openly sharing whatever unique, winning qualities you may possess.

PART FOUR

CHARISMA IN ACTION

How to Be a Winner at Love: Using Charisma to Find Love and to Build Relationships That Work

*At its best, loving becomes
one with the joy of living.*

We have been told what love is, how much we all want it, how lonely life can be without it, where to look for it, how to know when we have found it, how to make it good, and how to make it last — yet, we still have great difficulty in searching for it, finding it, capturing it, and sustaining it.

What else can you do after you've read all the books you can find on meeting and dating, on love, and on improving relationships? You know all the right things to do and have tried them, but still, you do not have the exciting relationship you want.

Although such efforts as practicing conversational skills, improving one's appearance, applying intimacy training, learning how to fight fair, and experimenting with the newest sexual techniques can help to develop more satisfying relationships, they cannot create heart-swelling, soul-stirring, life-enhancing, lasting love without some other all-important, basic ingredients.

LOVE'S MAIN INGREDIENT

The main ingredient of love is the person who experiences it. Our relationships with others are reflections of our relationship with ourselves. If we are happy with ourselves, we stand a good chance of being happy with someone else. If we love ourselves unconditionally, we are capable of unconditionally loving another. And if we are accepting, compassionate, forgiving, respectful, and supportive of ourselves, so we are likely to be with loved ones. Our loves are extensions of our approach to life. They are only as full, rich, and deep as we are as individuals.

The sweetness of love cannot easily weather the bitter environment of negative living. Those individuals who are critical, judgmental, and uncaring toward themselves or are similarly down on life are usually unsuccessful at love. Basing relationships on neurotic needs and voids in one's personality or life dooms them to be less than they could be, at best. Often they become destructive to one's well-being, bringing out the worst aspects of a person's personality.

All of the elements needed to find love and to sustain it at its best are highly developed in charismatic people. The very qualities that comprise their charisma also make them winners at love.

Charismatic individuals have a sense of inner security which allows them to comfortably risk rejection in search of love and, once having found it, to love confidently and unrestrainedly — willing to chance tomorrow's possible losses in order to experience the fulfillments of today. They choose partners with high levels of self-esteem similar to their own, making their relationships likely to be freer of demands, restrictions, tensions, and internal problems than they would be if self-esteem levels were lower. And truly liking themselves allows such persons to risk true intimacy — to become fully visible to their partners, unafraid of exposing sensitive or feared parts of their personalities. The self-esteem that is the very basis of charisma is also central to love.

Charismatic individuals have great capacity to love and to be loved. They give freely of themselves from depths many people never know exist. They notice, appreciate, and respond to sources of enjoyment most others take for granted, making them especially desirable partners. They savor every glance, touch, and emotion and use this heightened ability to extract joy from simple, everyday experiences to enhance their feelings of love. Their on-going efforts to achieve personal growth and expansion contribute to the growth and expansion of their relationships. And their zest for living, gaiety of spirit, spontaneity, and pursuit of that which is novel makes them fun, interesting, and different, thereby attractive to prospective lovers and stimulating to existing ones.

THE CHARISMATIC APPROACH TO FINDING LOVE

Don't expect love to create happiness.

Sometimes people use love as a lifeboat to save them from facing themselves. But love cannot rescue anyone. Don't expect it to make you feel better about yourself or to make your life better. It can make you feel valued but cannot create that value. And it can make more enjoyable a life that is already good, but it cannot transform an empty life into one that is full and rewarding. A relationship entered into with the belief underlying it that love brings happiness is built on quicksand. The momentary bliss soon gives way to the reality of pre-existing, everyday dissatisfactions. The lover is then often blamed for being lacking. Love is no substitute for personal happiness; it can only enhance it where it already exists.

A person who desperately seeks love most often hungers not for love but for self-esteem. Such an individual broadcasts his or her neediness. The look of one who has a burning desire to meet that "special person" is well recognized by others and sends them scurrying away in droves. Just as job offers that come when we are already employed seem to dry up when we are unemployed, so love usually comes when we are not looking so intently for it.

In the best pairings, we fall for those who reflect what we love in ourselves. They bring out and nurture the best parts of us. The ideal love relationship is based on an appreciation and celebration of oneself, of one another, and of life.

Know what you want in an ideal mate and be worthy of that person.

When searching for a love partner, it is important to know what you really want and what you don't want. Think about which positive qualities are of highest priority to you, which have less significance, and which have little or none. Consider which negative ones you could accept and which you could not.

Do you possess the positive qualities that you desire in someone else? What about the negative ones that you don't want? The surest way to attract an ideal mate is to be one. Most often winners choose other winners and losers choose other losers.

Don't look for perfection.

The pursuit of perfection is the enemy of the single person. It stops many potentially good relationships before they ever begin.

Keep an open mind and give new acquaintanceships some time to develop before deciding they aren't worth continuing. Usually an individual's desirable inner qualities are not immediately apparent. The vibrations we feel upon first meeting new people are unreliable for evaluation of future relationships. Some of the best pairings begin with the partners initially disliking one another. And many platonic friendships blossom into thriving love relationships. Love needs time to grow.

As masks come down and various characteristics are exposed, check them against your priority attributes. A suitable mate should possess the positive qualities of most importance to you and the negative ones, of which everyone has some, of least importance. Don't settle for less than what you want, but be realistic about what is attainable.

Although sound relationships are built upon having things in common, it is futile to search for someone who can relate to and satisfy every facet of your personality. It is burdensome to your partner and destructive to your relationship to expect any one individual to fulfill your every need. We are quite willing to have different friends to satisfy our varied interests — card friends, tennis friends, and close friends in whom we confide, for example. And we don't expect or need for our card friends to be our confidants, for instance. Yet often we want our love partners to share in every aspect of our beings although, realistically, no one ever can.

The charismatic person develops an effective support system — a network of relationships with friends and family members who supplement and complement those needs left unmet by his or her love partner. This eliminates the necessity of finding the "perfect" partner.

There is someone for everyone. Observe committed couples and you'll see individuals of every size, shape, and persuasion involved in relationships. It pays to be persistent.

Increase your exposure and take the initiative.

Social scientists say that we must meet 75 to 125 people in order to find one individual with whom we are truly compatible. To qualify as a "meeting," we must learn enough about the other person to determine whether or not compatibility might be possible. Brief hellos and superficial small talk are not considered sufficient.

The average person with low-to-moderate social skills may take two years or more to meet that one special person because he or she does not take advantage of everyday opportunities to meet new people and has difficulty expanding on those he or she does meet. It is quite a different story for charismatic individuals who go out of their way to be with others and for whom it is habitual to greet and to visit with many people throughout their daily routines and who are adept at turning brief meetings into new friendships.

Although they are highly approachable, charismatic people do not wait for others to make the first move. They decide whom they wish to meet and take the responsibility for making it happen. Those who wait for others to approach them risk meeting only those in whom they are not interested and chance missing good candidates who may, themselves, be reluctant to initiate an introduction. Do the choosing rather than waiting to be chosen.

Many ordinary places are excellent for meeting prospective love partners. The laundry room in an apartment complex is considered one of the best. The supermarket is another. And a line — any line — is great! If you see a line, get in it. Drift out a couple of steps, find someone ahead or behind you who looks interesting, and make an opening comment. People who are waiting for something are particularly easy to lure into conversation. For this reason, waiting rooms in professional offices, automobile repair establishments, and anywhere else where people are bored and have time to pass are especially good.

It is important to establish meeting opportunities in addition to everyday, unplanned exposures. Remember, the more people you meet, the sooner you will find the right one for you. Developing a people habit is the best cure for loneliness.

Go to places where people gather. The best ones are those which revolve around a common interest, such as hiking or sailing clubs, computer-user groups, or automobile shows. Auctions, trade shows, and classes all offer chances to meet individuals who like what you like. Whether you are into coins or mountain climbing, there are like-minded individuals who probably have planned activities in which you can participate. You will be doing what you enjoy while meeting others who like the same thing. But go for the fun of it — not to meet someone special. Then if you do not meet anyone, you will still enjoy the activity of your choice while increasing your knowledge and developing your social skills.

Having raised your exposure to people, the new goal becomes developing relationships. Make it a rule to extend or to accept at least one invitation each week. If no one asks you, you ask someone. Make no exceptions.

Have a positive dating attitude.

All too often dating is thought of as being an unpleasant screening procedure for the love of one's life. It is far preferable to view it as being an end in itself as it provides valuable opportunities to experience and to enjoy a variety of people.

Having a good time with someone who falls short of your ideal is a lesson in living fully — in making the most of everything. And it is often preferable to sitting home alone waiting for Mr. or Ms. Right. You may even meet your ideal mate while out with someone else.

APPLIED CHARISMA:
MAKING LOVE SPARKLE AND MAKING IT LAST

Have you ever wondered whether the kind of love you've always dreamed of is really possible? Whether the thrill of new love is inevitably replaced by comfort and ultimately by boredom? It doesn't have to be. There are people who enjoy the relationship you would like to have. Perhaps you've seen these happy couples — together for years and still very much in love. One can feel the chemistry between them when they look at one another. They didn't find the perfect partner and live happily ever after just by luck. Rather, they learned how to get the most from their relationship and then did the things that made and kept it special. They are living proof the dream of radiant, enduring love can come true. What is their secret? They have mastered the skill of loving — one we are seldom taught as we grow up. Fortunately, we can teach it to ourselves.

Charismatic individuals who pursue excellence in themselves and in life also actively strive for it in their relationships. They do not compromise their dreams of love, giving up excitement for security, freshness for reliability, or exhilaration for stability. They want the passion of love to enhance their lives just as their passion for life enhances their loves. Such people do not settle for lives of "quiet desperation" so common to those who remain in unnurturing, unfulfilling, dull love relationships — or worse.

Often, for such individuals, the dream of lasting, scintillating love has been deemed unrealistic. This is especially true of those who have repeatedly experienced the life and excitement eventually going out of previous long-term relationships.

The loss of loving feelings is a complex problem having numerous possible causes. The first step toward preserving exciting love is to recognize the major causes of its destruction.

Lack of knowledge or non-acceptance of one's partner.

The inability to accept the reality of who a partner really is once the relationship has progressed from the romantic, illusionary stage to one of real knowledge of each other is common. The large numbers of couples who divorce after about five years of marriage (and many others who wish they could have) often experienced loss of love as a result of either never succeeding in getting to know each other or of being unable to accept the person they came to know.

Men, notoriously, fall in love quicker than women, often stimulated by superficial attributes (usually physical), and they form stronger attachments than do most women, who usually take time to evaluate a potential partner before allowing themselves to become deeply involved.

Unfortunately, many love relationships are built on illusions and are overrun with expectations and demands. They revolve around ownership, obligations, and limitations that squelch personal freedom and smother loving feelings.

Once known and accepted, a love partner must be unconditionally loved in order for love to flourish. This means dispensing with the evaluative, qualifying attitude that originally helped to choose the partner and accepting and loving the whole person as he or she is — flaws and all.

Holding back feelings.

Holding back the complete truth from oneself or one's partner causes a person to lose the ability to feel positive emotions. Love is not the only victim. Passion disappears from all areas of life — joy, enthusiasm, and excitement, and, therefore, one's potential for charisma is also buried under the unresolved anger that inevitably results from denying and pushing down feelings. Burying our emotions eventually impoverishes our senses and makes us numb to life. A person will remain stuck at this undesirable emotional level until the accumulation of suppressed negative feelings are dealt with. Couples who have big fights over little issues have uncommunicated anger simmering below the surface. Inability to recognize and to express these negative feelings forge the sad fate of the relationship. When one partner becomes a scapegoat for the other's unfinished, unresolved personal business, the mounting resentment is devastating to love. No love is strong enough to withstand being used as a dumping ground for an individual's personal dissatisfactions, discontentments, anger with himself or herself, life situations or circumstances, or with his or her unresolved disappointments from the past.

A key to keeping love alive is to be aware of and to resolve conflicts and to communicate dissatisfactions on a daily basis. I'm passing along to you my mother's excellent advice given to me many years ago — never go to sleep feeling angry. Deal with whatever is upsetting you so each new day can begin with love.

Failure to feed loving feelings.

The biggest fear of part-time lovers everywhere all too often materializes — that with full-time commitment, especially marriage, passionate involvement will deteriorate to concerned interest and, ultimately, to disinterest. The humdrum nature of daily living and constant exposure to each other can sap the specialness from love — but only if it is allowed to. Familiarity can breed boredom and stop the growth of love unless loving feelings are regularly nourished. A relationship is a living process that needs tending. Proper feeding is essential to its survival.

NUTRIENTS OF LOVE — THE SUBSTANCE OF CHARISMA

Have you ever noticed the elusive way love can oscillate from being overwhelmingly intense to being nearly non-existent and then returning as if it had a mind of its own? You needn't succumb helplessly to love's whims. How we think and feel and what we say and do produces, maintains, augments, or diminishes our other emotions, and so it is with love. The power to create, sustain, and enhance loving feelings is yours to use as you wish.

An all-important goal in our relationships is to make love grow, thereby helping to draw out our untapped potential. When we nurture love, we expand our aliveness.

Think lovingly.

Just as focusing on the best, most exciting, and most fulfilling aspects of life can enhance our experience of living, concentrating on the best, most exciting, and most fulfilling aspects of love can enhance our experience of loving. How we feel about a love relationship depends upon our view of it. When love is at its peak and we are ecstatic, we see ourselves, our partners, and the world as wonderful, beautiful, and worthwhile. At these times we experience no negatives.

In order to achieve and maintain an extraordinary level of loving feelings, it is mandatory that couples focus as much as possible on each other's virtues and on the value of their relationship. When you think of your partner, remind yourself of his or her good points — the attributes that made you fall in love with him or her. Recall endearing habits and mannerisms, good experiences you have shared, and imagine future ones you have planned or hope for. Remember that your feelings are a result of what you think. Love is a natural emotional outgrowth of positive feelings about a person. If you focus on your partner's undesirable qualities, on times you have not gotten along well, or on plans that went awry, you will become aware that your loving feelings are waning.

See lovingly.

Candidly observe your partner while he or she is absorbed in activity, appreciating a favorite expression or taking notice of his or her most attractive physical features.

To remain special, feelings of love for a tired, bathrobed person who is stretched out on a couch watching television need to be periodically fueled by seeing him or her in positive roles other than that of being your partner.

Respect for and appreciation of his or her talents and abilities feed love. Make opportunities to see your loved one in work or recreational situations in which he or she particularly excels. Seeing your partner at his or her best through the eyes of admiring others enhances your feelings of love.

Feel lovingly.

Just as you can learn to make yourself feel happier, you can learn to make yourself feel more loving. Deliberately focus on and memorize the sensation of strong love and attempt to reproduce it at will. Once mastered, it can be used to exaggerate spontaneous loving feelings and to produce them when love ebbs.

Speak lovingly.

There is a psychological law that says whatever feelings you verbalize become stronger. Frequently expressing love and appreciation to your partner intensifies your experience of these emotions and it is vital to the health of your relationship. Everyone wants to feel special and this is particularly true in love relationships. Don't just *think* of your partner as being terrific — *tell* him or her. When you feel proud or especially like something he or she does or says, express it.

Love-robbing resentment easily results from having one's needs unmet. And love is increased when one partner fulfills a need of the other. But a person cannot read the mind of his or her partner to find out what those needs and desires are. Ask for what you want. Many a love has been extinguished by one or both partners neglecting to do so.

Show and share your inner self freely and become a friend to your partner's inner self. Becoming soul mates fulfills three of our greatest human needs — to be fully known, to be understood, and to be accepted by another human being. Relationships based on this link in inner lives are strong, resilient, and resistant to outside pressures.

Behave lovingly.

The loving behaviors that are so natural and effortless when one is newly in love all too often become less frequent or non-existent in long-term relationships. New love is expressed while, most often, old love is assumed. The cost is loss of aliveness in the relationship and diminishment of love. One should not be made to feel special only when love is new. Expression of adoration and appreciation need to be continued indefinitely.

Behaving lovingly toward a partner not only increases his or her feelings of love, but it enhances your own. Just as acting out a quality such as self-confidence makes one feel more self-confident, "acting as if" you are in love can increase your loving feelings. When loving feelings wane, pretending they are still strong can help to bring them back. And when they exist, but weakly, it can strengthen them.

How does one behave lovingly? Begin by applying the charismatic traits of thoughtfulness and attentiveness to love by doing the little things that cause love to grow. For instance, leave a love note on your partner's pillow, by the telephone, or in his or her lunch, purse, or automobile. Buy a gift when there is no special occasion except for celebration of your chosen "I-love-you" day. Send a loving card to his or her home or office (if marking it *confidential* will insure that it will be).

Alternate these notes with ones that share your excitement in being alive — cheerful drawings or sunny thoughts. Happy faces are especially effective on breakfast napkins and bathroom mirrors where they help to set a positive mood for the coming day.

Call on the telephone just to say, "I love you," "I miss you," or "I am thinking about you."

Another loving behavior evident in new relationships which diminishes in continuing ones is making physical contact. The warmth and closeness produced by touching one's partner enhances love, yet, as relationships mature, there is less and less touching in public places and in private ones.

Touch your partner's shoulder briefly as you walk by, hold hands, and walk arm in arm. Hugs and kisses not being used as non-verbal sexual invitations or requests are highly valued expressions of caring and tenderness.

Behaving lovingly also includes making time to have fun together, to make plans, to set goals, and to work on joint projects of mutual interest. A couple either builds together or grows apart. Marriage counselors report lack of playtime together as one of the major problems in numerous troubled relationships. There is a psychological principle that says you will be associated with what you experience together. It can be either enjoyment or mundane chores and everyday pressures — the choice is yours.

CHARISMA IN THE BEDROOM
CAPTURING THE SIZZLE

Charismatic individuals approach sex as they approach life — freely, confidently, and enthusiastically. And they savor sex as they savor life, focusing on the enjoyment of the process rather than becoming totally absorbed in only bringing about an end result.

No one is better equipped to enjoy sex than charismatic persons. Maximizing pleasure comes naturally to them. Their propensity to get caught up in the pleasure of the moment carries over from other areas of their lives into their sexual activities. Focusing on pleasurable sensations, one of the basics of sex therapy, is a spontaneous, everyday function of charismatic individuals. The passion they feel for living spills over into their sex lives. And they are in the habit of openly and fully expressing their emotions rather than holding them back (out of fear or guilt) as some people do when involved in sexual activity. They take their spontaneous, fun-loving, adventuresome natures to bed. Their high level of self-esteem makes it comfortable for them to drop all masks and to pridefully expose their real inner selves, the source of their charismatic power. Their huge capacity to give and to receive love, their sensitivity and responsiveness to the needs of others, their caring natures, and their ability to communicate effectively all contribute to the immense fulfillment charismatic individuals are capable of deriving from their sexual lives.

As you work on your Charisma Development Program, ridding yourself of old inhibitions and restrictions and become more self-assured and free to be yourself, you will increasingly experience sex as a life-affirming, natural high to which you are entitled — the ultimate celebration of yourself, of your life, and of your love for another.

KEYS TO GREAT SEX

Full sexual fulfillment requires:

Self-knowledge — knowing what arouses you, what your sexual preferences are, and what it takes for you to reach orgasm. And knowing what you dislike and what turns you off.

Self-acceptance — believing that you are a worthwhile person who is deserving of pleasure. Knowing that your sexual preferences and responses are uniquely yours and feeling that they are acceptable. Accepting your body as being lovable. And having sufficient self-esteem to let down all masks and to joyfully expose the real you to another person.

Acceptance of sexual activity as being good — believing sex to be a natural expression of one's humanness, a pure and beautiful gift from nature meant to be enjoyed.

Focusing — being able to enhance pleasurable sensations by focusing on them and by visualizing whatever is most arousing to you, undistracted by outside thoughts and concerns and unencumbered by inhibitions, self-consciousness, guilt, fears, or preconceived notions of how it "should" be.

Communication — saying or showing what you want, for, contrary to popular opinion, no matter how much your partner may love you, he or she does not automatically know what you like. You must take the responsibility for your own enjoyment. And the best lovers convey their enjoyment to their partners. Probably nothing is more exciting than a highly aroused lover. He or she validates one's manhood or womanhood. Genuine communication flares passion. The penalty for not expressing feelings is repressed anger that can prevent you from having satisfying sexual experiences.

A fulfilling sexual life adds a special, irreplaceable element to living, rounding out a person's range of pleasures and producing a sense of well-being that adds to one's charismatic power. Development of your charismatic qualities will help you to enhance your experience of all aspects of living, including the ability to derive maximum enjoyment from your sexual self.

Chapter Fourteen

Winning in the Work Place: Charisma, Salesmanship, Management, and Success

The most priceless commodity in the marketplace is charisma. It is in short supply and in high demand; its future is strong and its returns spectacular.

Applying the principles of charisma to business gives an individual that extra edge that can propel him or her to the pinnacle of success. Perhaps in no other area is charisma more directly related to achievement than in the work place where those who have self-confidence, an optimistic and enthusiastic attitude, pride in a job well done, and the ability to bring out the best in others quickly climb to the top in any field.

THE PRODUCT IS YOU

We are all selling ourselves all the time — our ideas and ambitions, our desires and needs, our skills and experience, and our products and services. The wife who hints that she would like to see a movie, a person asking another for a date, an individual on a job interview, and an employee asking the boss for a raise are all selling just as surely as those who are selling vacuum cleaners, office supplies, or medical or legal services. Regardless of what we are selling at any given moment, the basic product is ourselves.

What determines who will sell most successfully? The same charismatic characteristics that make people winners in their personal lives also make them winners in business. Their manner, attitude, approach, and appearance all affect their ability to persuade, to convince, and to win over others.

THE REAL SECRET OF SUCCESS

Advertising agencies fail to return telephone calls to million-dollar clients. Writers offered publishing contracts never produce the manuscripts. Deliveries are made after the promised date, if at all, and delivery people are unable to give you any idea when they will be coming (when they finally do, the merchandise is damaged or turns out to be someone else's order). Taxi drivers ask how to get to a certain address. Store clerks say, "If it isn't out, we don't have it." Repaired items are returned unfixed or have more problems than they did before being sent out. Offices are filled with workers listening to radio talk shows and lamenting, "Who can stand just to work all day?" Nurses do not let you know until after you arrive for your doctor's appointment that they never received your blood tests and x-rays from the lab. And complaints of poor service are met with excuses or snippy reproaches.

Perhaps it is foolish to expect things to be done properly. Inefficiency and poor attitude seem to be the watchwords of the day. The cry of employers everywhere is, "It's so hard to get good help these days." And, generally, this appears to be true. Many potential employees want high salaries and expect extensive employee-benefit packages, but few of them give top quality work in return. All too often above-standard compensation is paid for substandard work.

The good news is that the lackadaisical, slipshod, who-cares attitude which afflicts much of the work force creates fabulous opportunities for competent, efficient, follow-through type people who put forth their best effort and take old-fashioned pride in a job well done. If, in addition, they have a positive attitude communicated with energy and enthusiasm, the impact on people's assessment of them and what they have to offer is powerful. It instills confidence that boosts sales of products and services, and imbues belief in their abilities that creates unlimited new opportunities for business growth. It helps them to obtain jobs, to keep them, and to get promoted. And it aids them in getting customers and in sustaining their loyalty.

Such rare, desirable individuals are sought after, highly valued, and richly rewarded in business. They have doors open to them that are closed to others. There is little real competition for outstanding people in the business world. Those who "have it" usually make it. No field is too crowded for them. The lower and middle ranks may be impacted with those who are less motivated, less energized, less diligent, and less capable of selling themselves, but there is nearly always room at the top for individuals who make the most of their abilities and creativity by applying themselves wholeheartedly to work they love.

Charles Lazarus, founder and chairman of Toy's "R" Us, Inc., the country's largest and fastest growing toy retail chain, believes his biggest single advantage over most of his competition is that he loves what he does every day. It is not just a means to an end.

Successful fashion designer Holly Harp, who was also the driving force behind a $750,000-a-year Hollywood retail store, Holly's Harp, defines success as the ability to have joy and enthusiasm in what you are doing. She compares her work to a kid playing with mudpies.

Computer whiz Stephen Wozniak also considered his work to be play. He spent thousands of evening hours doing what he loved — designing a computer he really wanted. The result was the Apple computer that made him $50-million dollars.

The list of winners who see their work as play is endless. For these people, working hard is synonymous with playing hard. They do what they do for the satisfaction of it. The monetary rewards most often are simply the result of a game well played.

Success is usually the result of taking advantage of the chances you create for yourself. The good luck and opportunities you may have been looking for are likely to materialize when you take a charismatic approach to business.

WHAT DOES IT TAKE TO EXCEL IN SALES?

Sales are what business is all about. I first realized this while still a child selling Girl Scout cookies and magazine subscriptions for school drives. Later, as I worked my way through high school and college selling everything imaginable, including men's, women's, and children's clothing, housewares, plumbing and paint supplies, sporting goods, stationery and gift items, books, and health foods, I met business people who did not have the foggiest notion of how to maximize sales — the total producer of their revenue. This was equally true of those in charge of both small specialty stores and large chain operations.

Having been surrounded by salespersons ever since I can remember — from my very early childhood days of gift wrapping packages in my parent's retail stores to living as an adult with my sales-oriented family, I have been cognizant of those elements that increase sales and those that diminish them.

I observed my husband's transition from general manager of a large retail chain to a masterful independent wholesale salesman. In just a few years, Jerry built a widespread reputation for being one of the most admired, competent, and productive travelling salespersons in the women's apparel industry. In his showroom, every customer receives the same warm, genuine smile and friendly greeting, whether he or she represents one small store or a large chain. He knows their interests, concerns, and many of their families. He calls just to see how they are getting along when he knows they are going through difficult times, and he checks on the progress of ill children and spouses — all because he cares. Early on, new customers get the feeling they have joined his extended family.

Jerry's charismatic personality on the job provides an uplifting environment that makes working with him a pleasurable respite from the rest of the day. He freely uses his varied retail and buying experience and thorough knowledge of his lines to guide customers into buying patterns that maximize the profitability of their particular operations. And they know their welfare, friendship, and continuing loyalty are of higher priority to him than the dollar figure on any one order. As a result, some time ago when he changed his major line, his entire account structure remained nearly intact. And later, when he took on a new accessory line, he tripled the sales in the first year — thanks to the trust his people have in him. The powerful combination of a positive, caring attitude and skillfulness spell job satisfaction and big bucks for Jerry and for the companies he represents.

So we know that a grown man with an extensive business background and a charismatic approach to customers can excel in sales, but what are the chances of success for those individuals who are either new to selling and, perhaps, have not yet fully developed their skills or who are currently in sales and not doing as well as desired?

My son, Robbie, learned the answer to that question at the age of 12 on a day when he came home much earlier than usual from

selling flowers on a neighborhood corner. Not wanting to work
that morning, he had dejectedly watched dozens of cars stop at
the traffic signal and then continue on, their drivers apparently
not even noticing him walking back and forth with his bunches
of flowers. He became so bored, he decided to make a game of
capturing the eyes of drivers and of smiling broadly at them. To
those whose windows were open he enthusiastically said, "Beautiful
day to take some flowers to someone special, isn't it?" In just two
and one-half hours he sold out all of his flowers and nearly doubled
the amount he had received in tips the day before. Robbie quickly
learned the value of a positive attitude and a big smile as did a
13-year-old Virginia girl who set an all-time record and earned
the title of Girl Scout Cookie Queen by selling over $25,000 worth
(11,200 boxes) in only two months. How did she do it?

Firstly, she worked diligently at it every day after school and
on weekends. Secondly, convinced that she could break the existing record, she never lost sight of her goal. Thirdly, she maximized
her exposure to people who might buy her product by working
at the bottom of escalators in crowded subways and at bus stops
during rush hours.

In a *Los Angeles Times* article, this pixieish sales dynamo said
that her mother told her to "Look them in the eye, talk to them
personally, and speak up." And so she did — saying to men who
were walking with ladies, "Show you care! Buy Girl Scout cookies;"
to armed service personnel, "Fly with Girl Scout cookies;" or
"Bring some back for your shipmates." And she handled objec-
tions and dodges masterfully. She would say, "They're tax-
deductible. We take checks." And when someone took out a check,
she would add, "Why not buy a whole case?" If people replied
that they could not eat that many, she would say, "You can freeze
them."

Obviously, even a child who has a winning attitude and a skillful
approach can rack up some pretty impressive sales figures.

FOUR KEYS TO SALES EXCELLENCE
Four of the most important elements of top-notch selling are:
1. Thorough knowledge of the product
A salesperson who has only limited or no knowledge of his or
her product is at a marked disadvantage in representing it to a
potential customer. It is imperative that the seller be able to relate
the product's advantages, varied applications, proper use, limita-

tions, and possible dangers, if any. When such information is unavailable, people are usually more hesitant to buy. In order for a prospect to want to purchase a product, he or she must know enough about it to determine its desirability.

2. Sincere belief in the product and enthusiasm for it.
Represent products you believe to be good and use them yourself. Try competitor's products for comparison, taking notice of their advantages and disadvantages. See firsthand which things are better about your brand so that when you tell a customer your product will best fill his or her particular need, you honestly believe it to be true. If you are selling a spot remover that is more effective than any other you have ever tried, a facial cream that has improved your own appearance so much that friends are commenting about how vibrant and youthful you look lately, or an engine treatment that boosted your automobile gas mileage — your excitement about the product will instill in customers real confidence in its capability and value that can translate into big sales.

3. Responsiveness to the customers' needs.
No matter how marketable your product may appear to be, actual sales will result only when individuals perceive how it will improve their life styles, help them to feel or to look better, simplify or expedite a task or chore, or solve a particular problem. A salesperson's job is to service the needs of his or her customers. A charismatic person is in an excellent position to find out what those needs are. Warmth, openness, and friendliness create an atmosphere in which a prospect's desires and underlying motivations for buying can be exposed. Motivation to buy is created by helping the customer to perceive your product as fulfilling his or her particular need and doing it better, easier, faster, and/or cheaper than other similar products.

4. A positive, helpful, caring attitude toward customers.
People react negatively to salespeople who focus more intently on sales slip or purchase order totals than on how to best serve their needs, or who are uninterested in the transaction altogether. In such circumstances, potential customers are reticent to buy even if the product appears to be just what they need. People dislike being treated impersonally and resent feeling that they are being taken advantage of.
Your honesty and concern for your customers' welfare and satisfaction are apparent when it is uppermost in your mind to help satisfy their needs in the best way possible. The most likely

way to insure a sale is to give your customers reason to trust and to like you.

CHARISMA IN THE SERVICE PROFESSIONS

Perhaps more than in any other type of business, those in the service professions must have the ability to instill confidence in what they do to make people feel comfortable and safe in availing themselves of it.

Many a physician who has an outstanding bedside manner — a warm and caring attitude toward patients — develops a flourishing practice while some of his or her more highly skilled counterparts do not. A physician is in a unique position not only to stave off and to relieve much physical pain and suffering but also to prevent a great deal of pointless worry and anxiety. A little tender loving care goes a long way toward putting one's fears to rest. The doctor we "just love" and confidently recommend to friends and family is the one who takes the time and expends the effort to give it, realizing that being sensitive and responsive to a patient's emotional needs and well-being is as important a part of being a good doctor as is the mastering of diagnostic and treatment skills.

It is likewise important for other service professionals, such as dentists, attorneys, accountants, interior decorators, and beauticians, to be understanding and sympathetic to the concerns of those who come to them. Service people are running businesses not unlike those that market products and, basically, the same principles of success apply to them both.

CHARISMA IN SMALL BUSINESS

What makes one business thrive while another withers when their locations, the services they offer, and the prices they charge are virtually the same? I was asked this question recently by the puzzled owner of an automobile-repair shop whose business was barely staying in the black while a repair shop across the street from his usually appeared to have more customers than it could possibly handle.

The answer is that Leonard, the owner of the less successful shop, did not like being in the auto-repair business and he did not like his customers, either. His shop was situated in an affluent area, and he particularly resented the attitude of his women customers whom he said were "spoiled rotten." His feelings were quite apparent. He seemed to be doing them a favor to work on their cars. And when any of them complained about the prospect of being without an automobile, Leonard would impatiently ask, "Well, are you going to leave it or not?"

But everyone in the area knew and loved his busy competitor, John. He was a people lover who made an effort to remember every customer's name and to use it whenever he or she came in. He greeted each with a captivating smile that seemed to light up the whole garage. John got to know his customers, their concerns, and their schedule demands. He often loaned out his own car to those who had a carpool to drive or errands to run while he worked on their cars. Customers enjoyed their contact with him and considered him a friend who would gladly go out of his way to accommodate them. His entire business was built on referrals by his customers to their friends. And every new customer became loyal to him, returning again and again. Word-of-mouth is incredibly powerful. There is no advertisement in the universe as effective as a recommendation by a friend. It builds huge businesses and booming professional practices.

When charismatic principles are incorporated into the running of a small business, the positive results can sometimes be surprising. My parents, for example, owned and operated a chain of ladies' retail apparel stores. A number of years ago when they sold all but one, many loyal customers (some who had been shopping with them for 15 to 30 years) began to commute long distances to shop in their one remaining store. Although the selection was excellent, it is not what kept customers coming back. They came because of the way they were treated.

Knowing that people often rely upon them as fashion experts, saleswomen develop and share their abilities to coordinate and to accessorize outfits. And they are honest about how garments fit and look. Shoppers feel secure that they are purchasing clothing that is appropriate, stylish, and flattering to them. It is store policy for employees to go out of their way to accommodate special orders and to fill customer's special needs, even when doing so requires my parents to make extra trips downtown to showrooms or to manufacturers' factories to locate and to obtain a particular item needed in a hurry by someone for a gift, a trip, or a special occasion. Once again we see how treating people as special is handsomely rewarded in business.

How can a small toy store succeed in the face of malls and discount chains? There is a neighborhood toy store in a small suburb of Los Angeles that has become a Chanukah and Yuletide institution in spite of 20 years of stiff competition. Many customers who used to buy for their children are now buying for their grandchildren. The proprietors attribute their success to personal service and to their love of children.

Every child who walks in the door is greeted immediately. Anyone who has been in the store previously is known by name and past purchases and preferences are remembered. Parents can safely leave children to wander around and look, knowing that store personnel will keep an eye on them, patiently answer their questions, and encourage them to make their own choices — never attempting to influence or to pressure them.

The owners of the store have developed friendships with these children that span an entire generation. They have seen their tiny customers grow into adults who still shop in the place that has become a beloved part of their lives — a link to the past rich with memories and a present opportunity for new memories in the making.

Charisma on the sales floor has increased profitability and guaranteed the staying power of many small businesses and has turned others into mushrooming giants.

HOW SMALL BUSINESSES MAKE IT BIG

How can small, independent businesses compete with the chains whose centralized distribution and volume buying allow for lower prices, and whose diversity in merchandising creates superior selections?

They do it by being creative in offering unusual, distinctive services that are unavailable from their competitors and by concentrating on giving outstanding, personalized customer service. They create an atmosphere that makes the customer feel confident that his or her needs will be cheerfully, eagerly, and effectively met. This requires having adequate sales personnel on the retail floor who are knowledgeable about the stock and who are excited about what they do. Never underestimate the influential power of a prompt greeting, a polite, informed answer to a question, and a sincere "Come back soon" accompanied by a broad goodbye smile.

Happy, efficient salespeople make for satisfied customers who return again and again and send in their friends. These repeat customers and referrals are the mainstay of any business. Cultivating a good customer is like setting up an annuity. It pays over and over again. The top priority of owners of businesses on the way up should be not only to train and to motivate salespeople to sell effectively, but to create congenial work conditions in which each employee is treated with respect and a positive environment that provides ample opportunities for creative expression of an employee's individuality and personal growth. In such an atmosphere, charisma blossoms and, most often, so does business.

CHARISMA AND CHAIN STORES

Outstanding chain stores combine the best of both worlds — the strength and expertise of the chains with the warmth and personalized service of the independents. One has only to walk into a Nordstrom store to see this rare combination functioning in concert. This highly profitable store chain has a complete and diverse inventory, appealingly displayed. At any time, almost any item of apparel or accessory can be found to suit one's preference.

Sales personnel are plentiful, well acquainted with the stock, and friendly and eager to help customers. They increase their sales and make shopping considerably easier by taking customers from one department to another, or by bringing merchandise from other departments to the shopper — quickly locating desired items and writing them all up on one sales slip. They make an effort to remember the names of regular customers, keep records so they can telephone when an item of particular interest to them comes in, and efficiently and gladly follow through on special requests. The manager of the jewelry department of the San Fernando Valley store in Los Angeles once called all of her key vendors in an effort to find a particular style and color earrings that I wanted for a special occasion. Upon learning they were unavailable, she had several companies send similar styles for my perusal. She called me the day she spoke to her vendors and again when the earrings arrived at her store. Few department store chains provide such extensive customer service.

How does Nordstrom motivate its many employees and sustain its positive, customer-oriented attitudes? When hired, each employee is given an intake packet which includes a diagram of the corporate structure. The inverted pyramid, which is also prominently displayed on the walls in employee-only areas, clearly recognizes the customer-salesperson transaction as the company's number one priority.

C U S T O M E R S

SALES & SALES SUPPORT PEOPLE

DEPARTMENT MANAGERS

STORE MANAGERS & BUYERS
MERCHANDISING MANAGERS

BOARD OF DIRECTORS

Although the desirability of this hierarchy is given abundant lip service by most companies, only a handful of them actually live it.

Nordstrom salespeople are paid salaries well above the average rate for the retail clerk industry, helping the company to attract and to keep quality people. Positive reinforcement is abundant, incentive programs are continuous, punishments and formal reprimands are virtually non-existent, and inspirational department and regional meetings are frequent. Ideas originating at the sales level are encouraged and considered seriously. And any negative people who somehow may manage to infiltrate the company soon drop out or are weeded out, maintaining the integrity of the positive work environment.

The same elements that make Nordstrom a winner across the board can also make particular stores outstanding within a large chain — sometimes doing five or six times more in sales than the other stores.

Automated, highly structured policies and merchandising formats can make all the stores within any chain somewhat the same. Some specialty store chains even issue weekly photographs of displays which are to be duplicated exactly, making all their stores virtually identical. So what could possibly make some store's sales so far exceed the others?

Enthusiasm is the one element common to top producing stores. When a manager who possesses generous amounts of it also knows how to arouse it in others, the entire store crackles with the excitement of salespeople who love their work and who are eager to help customers. This positive energy dramatically increases sales.

Extensive, innovative recognition programs are used by managers of top stores to help sustain the enthusiasm. And an employee's self-expression is encouraged in areas left unrestricted by company mandates and tight controls.

Once again, charisma makes the difference between excellence and mediocrity.

CHARISMA AND BIG BUSINESS
THE MANAGEMENT PHILOSOPHY OF WINNERS

People, more than any other factor, are what make a business succeed or cause it to fail. They can be its primary asset or most debilitating liability. Therefore, the continuous growth, development, and happiness of a company's people should be a top priority.

Many of the most highly successful companies have attained their enviable status by bringing to life a people-oriented business philosophy — a style of management that is much talked about in business circles though not yet widely practiced in its entirety. It is the ultimate effort to help people to develop their full potential for their own good and for the good of the company. It is a philosophy that accepts everyone as being special and capable of making an important contribution. It is responsive to the needs of the whole person to feel good about himself or herself and about what he or she does, and it emphasizes providing a supportive environment in which each individual is encouraged and helped to grow professionally and personally and to be happy and fulfilled as a human being. Adherence to this philosophy has proven to bring out the best that people have to give and put it to work to the great advantage of the company.

Practicing a people-oriented philosophy has allowed Olga Company, one of the most successful apparel businesses in the country, to set annual after-tax profit records for most of its 44 years in existence.

Jan Erteszek, Olga's chairman and chief executive officer (CEO), believes that the "hired hand" concept of labor is obsolete and destructive to man's dignity. He accepts that the total person becomes a member of the company and the total person must be served by it. From the beginning, Erteszek has employed a strategy called the "common venture enterprise" which stresses the team effort and equal value to the success of the company of every individual employee, regardless of position. Each person is respected, listened to, and has his or her problems dealt with.

Other people-oriented companies such as 3M, Hewlett-Packard, Texas Instruments, and IBM are comprised of work forces that are respected, treated as a valuable source of ideas, and recognized as the root origin of quality and productivity gain.

Knowing that employees' latent abilities and creative thinking are a major resource for any company, the president and CEO of IBM Corporation encourages employees to stretch themselves — to bravely take that step forward into uncharted territory. He provides a safety net for their inevitable failures when they occur, giving his people more than one chance to prove that his belief in them is well-founded.

When people are seen as being capable, they strive to live up to that expectation to the benefit of everyone.

Eagerness to encourage its people to translate their individuality and entrepreneurship into corporate gains is a goal of increasing numbers of companies. Intel Corporation, a leader in microelectronics, employs network management in favor of the usual hierarchical structure. This means that the communication barriers inherent in hierarchies are non-existent. Rather than being made by one leader, decisions are arrived at by a triad of executives. Workers may have several bosses and/or be responsible to committees that oversee various company functions. Employees at all levels are treated as equals and are encouraged to freely participate in discussions and to challenge superiors. The work environment is informal in dress and in physical arrangement. Instead of traditional offices, Intel people have designated work areas separated only by shoulder-high partitions. Everything possible is done to remove visible reminders of rank. In such an atmosphere, obstacles to charismatic interaction on the job are removed.

Many forward-looking executives in the corporate community are applying charismatic principles. Expansion of their concern for employee general welfare has prompted PepsiCo, Exxon, Zerox, Chase Manhattan, and Mobil Oil to be among 500 other corporations that have instituted wellness centers which offer physical-fitness programs overseen by full-time directors. Increasingly, entrepreneurs are being encouraged to develop new ventures within the corporate framework. And the old corporate hierarchy is giving way to a new lateral structure which takes advantage of input and expertise from all sectors.

Although many companies ascribe to fragmented aspects of a people-centered business philosophy, few apply it as widely or are as passionately devoted to it as is Mary Kay Ash, founder and CEO of Mary Kay Cosmetics. This remarkable company, doing over $300 million per year with over 2,000 sales consultants, is known worldwide for its people orientation.

Mary Kay's approach to management is based on the Golden Rule — "Do unto others as you would have them do unto you." The needs, desires, feelings, and happiness of her people are her top priority. Mary Kay says that to her, P and L doesn't mean only profit and loss — it also means people and love.

When she started the company, Mary Kay's dream was to enrich the lives of everyone who worked for her, emotionally and spiritually as well as financially. She professes a hierarchy of priorities for her people — God first, family second, and career third. When people live by a well-defined set of personal standards that accentuate belief and brotherhood, and when they have their family lives in order and family members solidly behind them, their business life is enhanced for their energies are free to be channeled into their work.

There are no separate executive lunch or restrooms in the elaborate Mary Kay corporate office building in Texas. An open-door policy provides access to top management that, in any corporation, is critical to smooth functioning and serves as a safeguard against the occurrence of Watergate-type incidents. The atmosphere is friendly and relaxed. There are no titles on executive doors and everyone is addressed by their first names.

The Mary Kay organization is like a big family, each member of which is expected to help the others to grow and to prosper — and virtually must do so in order to succeed in the company. Not only are Mary Kay people given the opportunity to succeed, they are taught how and then helped to do it.

A job well done is more than just recognized, appreciated, and praised — it is richly rewarded. Pink Cadillacs, mink coats, diamond bumblebee pins, and fabulous trips abroad that include first-class passage, hotels, dining, and limousine escorts are awarded to high achievers at annual three-day seminars with much pomp and ceremony in front of large audiences. Everything the company does is first rate, giving workers a feeling of importance — a confident, positive mind-set that nourishes the whole person and helps to motivate her to personal and business excellence.

CHARISMA AND THE EXECUTIVE IMAGE

A company develops a personality that reflects the traits of its chief executive officer. His or her attitude, physical presentation, and work ethics filter down through the ranks and establish the tone of the entire work environment. A capable, fair, dynamic CEO, who is also congenial, caring, positive, and enthusiastic, usually heads up a work force of efficient, hard-working, loyal, friendly, energetic people. Such a person extracts the optimum from his or her employees, for all leaders lead by example whether they want to or not.

During the Chrysler crisis, CEO Lee Iacocca's positive, never-say-die attitude, dedication to the survival of the company, and creative strategies marshalled employees behind him like eager troups behind General Patton. Ready to follow him anywhere, Iacocca's people stayed through pay cuts, demotions, and deep concerns about their uncertain futures — functioning as a team going for the win. Previously high absenteeism was cut by more than one half and a new spiritedness supplanted what had been pervasive indifference. He enlisted the help and gained the allegiance of Chrysler dealers by attending to their grievances and by inspiring them to join the massive team effort to save Chrysler. His charisma on television commercials made his name a household word and gave him the strong public support he sought. Even celebrities like Frank Sinatra, Bob Hope, Bill Cosby, and Pearl Bailey rallied behind him, donating time and effort to the cause.

Truly leading by example, Iacocca never expected any of his people to do anything he would not do himself. He demanded that they give their all only after *he* had made a total commitment. He cut his own annual salary to one dollar before cutting those of his employees. And he demands fierce loyalty, but also gives it.

Although generally known as a tough, uncompromising taskmaster, some men who have worked closely with Iacocca for over

35 years see him as a "softie" under that hard-nosed exterior. They have described him as a kind, very gentle, caring man. He has a sharp wit and a way with people. He sees setbacks as things that can become positives if he applies himself, and he has the ability to visualize a need and to fill it long before others even realize it exists. Iacocca is a spellbinder who has used his charisma to achieve what many people thought was an impossible task — the salvaging of Chrysler.

Contrary to popular belief, "nice guys" do not always finish last in business. Some of the most successful CEOs are charismatic individuals whose strengths and dynamism are tempered by kindness and whose directness and decisiveness are softened by sensitivity. These qualities serve to propel their companies to monumental heights.

An excellent example of executive charisma in action is Mary Kay Ash who virtually has become a beloved institution. Recently at the Governor's Conference on Women in Business held in Los Angeles, Mary Kay was among those who spoke before an audience of 2,000 women. They excitedly cheered and applauded her. After her presentation, many ran up front to experience the thrill of shaking her hand or to get a treasured autograph.

Why is Mary Kay so respected and adored? She always has a smile for everyone she meets. She seems to care deeply about all of her people regardless of their position in the company. She gives them the hope of achieving their dreams, optimism about their ability to succeed, and fosters a nurturing climate in which the shy become confident, the plain become attractive, the inhibited become assertive, and the inexperienced become accomplished. Her enthusiasm and positive outlook on life permeate her entire company, strongly affecting the attitudes of her people. At all levels of management, the company is laced with those who mirror Mary Kay's manner of leadership. Her company's personality is a true reflection of this dynamic woman.

What does all this mean to Mary Kay Cosmetics? It means that every consultant experiencing a feeling of personal and company pride does her job enthusiastically and does it well, markedly increasing her own sales and, in turn, those of the company.

We tend to pattern ourselves after individuals we respect and try to please those whom we admire. But these rewards must be earned — they cannot be demanded. Unfortunately, all too many employees are contending with confrontational, harsh, demeaning bosses whose own inability to cope and whose ineptness as leaders cause them to behave in a manner that produces anxiety and resentment in their people. This poor treatment is met with resistance, for it is our nature to rebel against being coerced, badgered, or humiliated into performing. Most often such inexcusable treatment is repaid with a sabotaging of the work effort and environment. Company loyalty and pride are non-existent as negativity becomes the company watchword. Dog-eat-dog competition, political manipulation, and debilitating tension among employees seep out and poison customer relations as well. As morale fails, so does productivity, for it is nothing more than the collective effort of hundreds of thousands of individual employees whose motivation to achieve, or lack thereof, determines the quantity and quality of goods and services produced.

One can only get the best from people when they want to give it. A charismatic leader can create and continuously fuel this desire in others. Charismatic leadership provides a pipeline to company success.

THE FUTURE OF CHARISMA IN THE WORK PLACE

We are standing on the threshold of an exciting new era in which opportunities for charismatic individuals are unlimited. Well prepared to step confidently into new horizons, they are likely to grow and prosper when challenged by our evermore complicated technological society. And they have the potential to rise above the crowd in the highly competitive marketplace of the future by capitalizing on their outstanding work habits and unique ability to win people over.

Although we have always responded to the warmth, vibrance, and personal touch of the charismatic person, the cold, impersonal nature of our new high-technology age makes us hunger for it more than ever. The more time we spend working on emotionless computers and talking to unfeeling unanswering machines, the more we value the charismatic individual who lifts us out of this technological vacuum and into the realm of experience, of stimulation, and of human connectedness. Those who have this ability to balance out our new world will find a very special place for themselves within it.

PART FIVE

YOUR OWN "SPECIAL MAGIC"

Chapter Fifteen

Your Personal Charisma Development Plan

*See each step as an exciting challenge,
each success as an ultimate achievement,
each day as a new beginning — and your
dreams will materialize before your eyes.*

If you are excited by the thought that you can have charisma, you are already on your way to possessing it. But how many times have you experienced a similar feeling and had nothing come of it? Frequently, perhaps after reading self-help books or attending motivational lectures, you were bursting with self-confidence, convinced that, this time, you would set the world on fire — only to find yourself left with nothing but smoldering embers by the next day. If you have had this happen to you, you know full well that dreams, enthusiasm, and a positive attitude, alone, are not enough. Results are achieved by a combination of desire, belief, know-how, and action.

Whether or not you actually develop charisma depends, first, upon your making a firm decision to do whatever is necessary to attain it. Doing so must become a high-priority goal in your life starting right now. And it is vital that you begin immediately. Most often, "later," "tomorrow," and "when I have more time" translate into "never." Overcoming the inertia to take that first step is always the most difficult part of undertaking any task or of achieving any goal.

If acquiring all the skills needed to develop charisma seems a bit overwhelming, remember that big goals are achieved by a series of small, steady, planned actions. Every nail counts toward building a house and every stitch puts one closer to a finished garment.

But unlike unfinished houses that cannot be lived in and unfinished garments that cannot be worn, charisma can be enjoyed early on and simply gets better — more natural, more effective, and more lasting as one continues to work at it. You need not wait until you have mastered all of the skills and techniques to experience the ecstacy of charisma or to derive massive benefits from it. There is no predetermined end to the infinite continuum of charisma development; no set time when it is attained so fully and completely that it cannot be improved upon. For most of us, the pursuit of powerful charisma becomes a valued, lifelong process of personal growth during which we reap rewards as we go along.

HOW TO IMPLEMENT THE CHARISMA DEVELOPMENT PROGRAM

In our fast-paced world of instant information, crash diets, and disposable relationships, we tend to seek out easy answers and immediate rewards. But charisma cannot be ingested in pill form nor can it be bestowed upon one with the wave of a magic wand. To attain charisma, you must want it passionately enough to put forth the sustained effort it requires. And although there are no shortcuts and immediate successes are rare, remarkable results frequently can be obtained in a surprisingly short period of time — often a few weeks to a few months. Thinking that you are too busy to do what it takes or that it seems like too much trouble to bother with will practically guarantee that you will not develop it at all.

Check your calendar and clock right now. Indelibly etch the date and the time in your mind. This moment marks the birth of a new you and the start of life as you so often may have wished it.

Take that first step along the road to fulfilling your charismatic potential by selecting one charisma-blocking belief, daily charisma-developing exercise, daily charisma-enhancing exercise, or charisma-sustaining behavior from Part II of this book, "Brightening Up the Inner You." Work on this belief or exercise until the desired attitude, feelings, and behavior become comfortable and automatic. This may take anywhere from a few days to several weeks. Then select a new belief or exercise to work on. For example:

DAILY CHARISMA-DEVELOPING EXERCISE #1
Make a list of your good qualities and past successes.

Read it at least three times a day.

Write your selection here.

_____

_____

_____

Next, select one category from Part III of this book, "Brightening Up the Outer You," either nonverbal communication, voice, conversational skills, or physical-image enhancement. Then choose a particular technique, skill, or task within that category. When mastered or completed, select a new item within the same category. Continue in this fashion until some degree of expertise is developed in the chosen category. Then select a new area of concentration and choose a technique, skill, or task in the new category. For example:

NONVERBAL COMMUNICATION
SOFTEN TECHNIQUES

Write your category selection here.

_____

Write your skill, technique, or task selection within that category here.

_____

_____

You will be working on one new item to develop the inner you and one to develop the outer you at any given time. In the beginning, choose assignments you feel will be beneficial to you but that are not extremely difficult or anxiety-producing. It is wise to give yourself a chance to experience some moderate successes before going for the big ones.

Refrain from the temptation to take on too much, too soon. Doing so is usually a fruitless exercise in frustration and, ultimately, can lead to abandonment of the entire program. Do not fall into the trap of becoming overzealous. Time after time, individuals who try too hard and go too fast in self-help endeavors, find it too difficult and, so, give up, justifying staying as they are by reasoning that they tried but the program was unworkable or too demanding. When used properly, the Charisma Development Program works. So, NO EXCUSES!

YOUR CONTRACT FOR SUCCESS

Vague goals are seldom achieved. Such desires as being more friendly, feeling better about oneself, or improving one's social ability are much too undefined to act on. To become attainable goals, they must be concrete — specific, measurable, and written down.

Some skills are best learned by breaking them down into their component parts or into sub-skills and practicing a different one each day or week. For example, if you are trying to learn the nonverbal SOFTEN signals, you might smile at five people the first day, add open posture the second day, a forward lean the third day and so on. By the sixth day, you will have integrated all six of the SOFTEN signals into your behavior. To attempt all six on the first day would be difficult to do.

Experimentation with various methods of organizing people's efforts to achieve maximum benefits from the Charisma Development Program has shown the importance of beginning each week by evaluating your previous week's progress and by planning new daily goals and recording them for easy reference onto a calendar which can be carried with you. For instance, if your selections for the week were to be the first charisma-developing exercise (Make a list of your good qualities and past successes. Read it at least three times a day.) and the nonverbal SOFTEN techniques, your calendar might look like this —

SUNDAY	MONDAY	TUESDAY	WEDNESDAY	THURSDAY	FRIDAY	SATURDAY
1 Progress Exercises	2 Make list S	3 Read list SO	4 Read list SOF	5 Read list SOFT	6 Read list SOFTE	7 Read list SOFTEN

As you complete your goals each day, it is appropriate to reward yourself with something that you enjoy. It can be participating in an activity you like — perhaps hitting golf balls at the driving range, going to a special restaurant, taking a walk, or simply soaking in the bathtub while listening to music. Wearing your best pajamas or cologne, spending some time with a favorite person, or buying a new record or book are also good rewards. And generously praise yourself for every effort, whether or not you consider the results to be successful. Winners are in the habit of congratulating themselves and feeling proud when they meet a goal, while losers usually criticize themselves for not doing better.

WHAT TO EXPECT AS YOU BEGIN TO CHANGE

We experience a particular feeling of comfort when we are "being ourselves." New behavior causes us to feel "unlike ourselves" and, therefore, uncomfortable. This initial strangeness is an expected part of the process of changing; yet, it causes many people to give up just when they are about to succeed.

We are strongly addicted to the image we have of ourselves, which a part of us fights to sustain — even if it is destructive. We perpetuate this self-image by continuously "proving" its accuracy. We do this in two ways. The first is by thinking and behaving in accordance with it. This means that if you consider yourself to be shy, every time you act shy you reinforce that feeling about yourself. However, if you act confident and outgoing, you begin to undermine the belief that you are a shy person. Eventually, the unsupported feelings fizzle out, the discomfort subsides, and your opinion of yourself changes.

The second way we keep our self-image intact is by interpreting what we see, hear, and do in such a way that it supports our current opinion of ourselves. If you consider yourself to be a poor math student, for example, and you receive a "D" on an examination, your grade will reaffirm your original opinion. It will be accepted as accurate and just what you deserved. But if you receive an "A" on an exam, you would probably decide you just "got lucky" or that the test was extremely easy, thus preserving your self-image as a poor math student.

We accept and are more likely to remember messages that agree with our self-image while we screen out conflicting ones, usually by minimizing or discounting them and quickly forgetting them

or by ignoring them altogether. This is why when our self-image
is poor, compliments are disbelieved or are fleeting while insults
seem true and can cause pain that lingers for long periods of time.

At first, it is often necessary to force yourself to use incoming
messages to support good feelings about yourself. Try to focus
on positive feedback that "proves" you are worthwhile, capable,
intelligent, attractive, interesting, and liked by others. Keep this
firmly in mind as you follow the Charisma Development Program,
and little by little the new you will emerge.

Although your new self-image will become self-perpetuating in
time, there is a strong tendency to slip back into old ways of react-
ing and relating. There is security in the familiarity of one's previous
self. Emotional growth is a two-steps-forward, one-step-backward
process. Each new plateau will be higher than the last and each
backslide less severe and/or lasting. Do not be afraid that something
is not working. Go with the ebb and flow, taking one step and
one day at a time. Keep your dream clearly in view of your mind's
eye and your expectations realistic, and wholeheartedly celebrate
every success, no matter how small it may seem.

Once you get caught up in the momentum of excitement that
comes from seeing results, you will become eager to try harder
and to do more. And as you acquire charismatic skills, they will
become easier and easier to sustain. In time, you will become able
to use and to benefit from them, effortlessly.

BELIEVE IN MAGIC

By now you are well aware that your present and future are not
automatically dictated by your past. You are not powerless to change
that which holds you back, prevents you from being the way you
want to be, or makes you feel unfulfilled or unhappy. Every day,
you choose to continue being the way you have been or to be different. No matter what you are like at this moment, you can have
"that special magic" by deciding right now to embrace it or you
can do nothing and let it slip away. You can exist until the end
of your days in a mundane world of your own creation ever wondering, "Is this all there is?" Or you can choose to experience the
delectable sense of adventure and the ecstasy that comes from being vibrantly and fully alive.

It is my fondest hope that one day soon you will experience
your own charisma, that you and everyone around you will see

its radiance shining in your eyes and that you will, from that day forward, feel it always filling your heart, your soul, and your life with its joyous magic.

A PERSONAL WORD FROM MARCIA GRAD

I am interested in hearing of the results you have obtained by using the material in this book. Feel free to write to me in care of my publisher. If you want answers to any questions, please enclose a self-addressed stamped envelope.

Periodically, I will conduct seminars in major cities throughout the country and on cruise ships. Should you want to be notified of these seminars, please write to me stating your interest.

Also, let me know if you would like to be placed on my mailing list to receive from time to time supplementary information in the form of a newsletter.

Lastly, consider ordering from Wilshire Book Company my three-hour Charisma Cassette Tapes. The tapes, recorded live at one of my seminars, will reenforce the material contained in this book. They sell for $25.00 plus $1.00 for postage and handling.

You can write to me at the following address:

Marcia Grad
c/o Wilshire Book Company
12015 Sherman Road
North Hollywood, California 91605-3781

A PERSONAL WORD FROM MELVIN POWERS
PUBLISHER, WILSHIRE BOOK COMPANY

Dear Friend:

My goal is to publish interesting, informative, and inspirational books. You can help me accomplish this by answering the following questions, either by phone or by mail. Or, if convenient for you, I would welcome the opportunity to visit with you in my office and hear your comments in person.

Did you enjoy reading this book? Why?

Would you enjoy reading another similar book?

What idea in the book impressed you the most?

If applicable to your situation, have you incorporated this idea in your daily life?

Is there a chapter that could serve as a theme for an entire book? Please explain.

If you have an idea for a book, I would welcome discussing it with you. If you already have one in progress, write or call me concerning possible publication. I can be reached at (213) 875-1711 or (818) 983-1105.

Sincerely yours,

MELVIN POWERS

12015 Sherman Road
North Hollywood, California 91605

MELVIN POWERS SELF-IMPROVEMENT LIBRARY

ASTROLOGY

____ ASTROLOGY: HOW TO CHART YOUR HOROSCOPE *Max Heindel*	5.00
____ ASTROLOGY AND SEXUAL ANALYSIS *Morris C. Goodman*	5.00
____ ASTROLOGY MADE EASY *Astarte*	5.00
____ ASTROLOGY, ROMANCE, YOU AND THE STARS *Anthony Norvell*	5.00
____ MY WORLD OF ASTROLOGY *Sydney Omarr*	7.00
____ THOUGHT DIAL *Sydney Omarr*	7.00
____ WHAT THE STARS REVEAL ABOUT THE MEN IN YOUR LIFE *Thelma White*	3.00

BRIDGE

____ BRIDGE BIDDING MADE EASY *Edwin B. Kantar*	10.00
____ BRIDGE CONVENTIONS *Edwin B. Kantar*	7.00
____ COMPETITIVE BIDDING IN MODERN BRIDGE *Edgar Kaplan*	7.00
____ DEFENSIVE BRIDGE PLAY COMPLETE *Edwin B. Kantar*	15.00
____ GAMESMAN BRIDGE—PLAY BETTER WITH KANTAR *Edwin B. Kantar*	5.00
____ HOW TO IMPROVE YOUR BRIDGE *Alfred Sheinwold*	5.00
____ IMPROVING YOUR BIDDING SKILLS *Edwin B. Kantar*	4.00
____ INTRODUCTION TO DECLARER'S PLAY *Edwin B. Kantar*	7.00
____ INTRODUCTION TO DEFENDER'S PLAY *Edwin B. Kantar*	7.00
____ KANTAR FOR THE DEFENSE *Edwin B. Kantar*	7.00
____ KANTAR FOR THE DEFENSE VOLUME 2 *Edwin B. Kantar*	7.00
____ TEST YOUR BRIDGE PLAY *Edwin B. Kantar*	5.00
____ VOLUME 2—TEST YOUR BRIDGE PLAY *Edwin B. Kantar*	7.00
____ WINNING DECLARER PLAY *Dorothy Hayden Truscott*	7.00

BUSINESS, STUDY & REFERENCE

____ CONVERSATION MADE EASY *Elliot Russell*	4.00
____ EXAM SECRET *Dennis B. Jackson*	3.00
____ FIX-IT BOOK *Arthur Symons*	2.00
____ HOW TO DEVELOP A BETTER SPEAKING VOICE *M. Hellier*	4.00
____ HOW TO SELF-PUBLISH YOUR BOOK & MAKE IT A BEST SELLER *Melvin Powers*	10.00
____ INCREASE YOUR LEARNING POWER *Geoffrey A. Dudley*	3.00
____ PRACTICAL GUIDE TO BETTER CONCENTRATION *Melvin Powers*	3.00
____ PRACTICAL GUIDE TO PUBLIC SPEAKING *Maurice Forley*	5.00
____ 7 DAYS TO FASTER READING *William S. Schaill*	5.00
____ SONGWRITERS' RHYMING DICTIONARY *Jane Shaw Whitfield*	7.00
____ SPELLING MADE EASY *Lester D. Basch & Dr. Milton Finkelstein*	3.00
____ STUDENT'S GUIDE TO BETTER GRADES *J. A. Rickard*	3.00
____ TEST YOURSELF—FIND YOUR HIDDEN TALENT *Jack Shafer*	3.00
____ YOUR WILL & WHAT TO DO ABOUT IT *Attorney Samuel G. Kling*	5.00

CALLIGRAPHY

____ ADVANCED CALLIGRAPHY *Katherine Jeffares*	7.00
____ CALLIGRAPHER'S REFERENCE BOOK *Anne Leptich & Jacque Evans*	7.00
____ CALLIGRAPHY—THE ART OF BEAUTIFUL WRITING *Katherine Jeffares*	7.00
____ CALLIGRAPHY FOR FUN & PROFIT *Anne Leptich & Jacque Evans*	7.00
____ CALLIGRAPHY MADE EASY *Tina Serafini*	7.00

CHESS & CHECKERS

____ BEGINNER'S GUIDE TO WINNING CHESS *Fred Reinfeld*	5.00
____ CHESS IN TEN EASY LESSONS *Larry Evans*	5.00
____ CHESS MADE EASY *Milton L. Hanauer*	5.00
____ CHESS PROBLEMS FOR BEGINNERS *Edited by Fred Reinfeld*	5.00
____ CHESS SECRETS REVEALED *Fred Reinfeld*	2.00
____ CHESS TACTICS FOR BEGINNERS *Edited by Fred Reinfeld*	5.00
____ CHESS THEORY & PRACTICE *Morry & Mitchell*	2.00
____ HOW TO WIN AT CHECKERS *Fred Reinfeld*	3.00
____ 1001 BRILLIANT WAYS TO CHECKMATE *Fred Reinfeld*	5.00

_____ 1001 WINNING CHESS SACRIFICES & COMBINATIONS *Fred Reinfeld*   7.00

COOKERY & HERBS

_____ CULPEPER'S HERBAL REMEDIES *Dr. Nicholas Culpeper*   3.00
_____ FAST GOURMET COOKBOOK *Poppy Cannon*   2.50
_____ GINSENG—THE MYTH & THE TRUTH *Joseph P. Hou*   3.00
_____ HEALING POWER OF HERBS *May Bethel*   4.00
_____ HEALING POWER OF NATURAL FOODS *May Bethel*   5.00
_____ HERBS FOR HEALTH—HOW TO GROW & USE THEM *Louise Evans Doole*   4.00
_____ HOME GARDEN COOKBOOK—DELICIOUS NATURAL FOOD RECIPES *Ken Kraft*   3.00
_____ MEDICAL HERBALIST *Edited by Dr. J. R. Yemm*   3.00
_____ VEGETABLE GARDENING FOR BEGINNERS *Hugh Wiberg*   2.00
_____ VEGETABLES FOR TODAY'S GARDENS *R. Milton Carleton*   2.00
_____ VEGETARIAN COOKERY *Janet Walker*   7.00
_____ VEGETARIAN COOKING MADE EASY & DELECTABLE *Veronica Vezza*   3.00
_____ VEGETARIAN DELIGHTS—A HAPPY COOKBOOK FOR HEALTH *K. R. Mehta*   2.00
_____ VEGETARIAN GOURMET COOKBOOK *Joyce McKinnel*   3.00

GAMBLING & POKER

_____ ADVANCED POKER STRATEGY & WINNING PLAY *A. D. Livingston*   5.00
_____ HOW TO WIN AT DICE GAMES *Skip Frey*   3.00
_____ HOW TO WIN AT POKER *Terence Reese & Anthony T. Watkins*   5.00
_____ WINNING AT CRAPS *Dr. Lloyd T. Commins*   5.00
_____ WINNING AT GIN *Chester Wander & Cy Rice*   3.00
_____ WINNING AT POKER—AN EXPERT'S GUIDE *John Archer*   5.00
_____ WINNING AT 21—AN EXPERT'S GUIDE *John Archer*   5.00
_____ WINNING POKER SYSTEMS *Norman Zadeh*   3.00

HEALTH

_____ BEE POLLEN *Lynda Lyngheim & Jack Scagnetti*   3.00
_____ DR. LINDNER'S SPECIAL WEIGHT CONTROL METHOD *Peter G. Lindner, M.D.*   2.00
_____ HELP YOURSELF TO BETTER SIGHT *Margaret Darst Corbett*   3.00
_____ HOW YOU CAN STOP SMOKING PERMANENTLY *Ernest Caldwell*   5.00
_____ MIND OVER PLATTER *Peter G. Lindner, M.D.*   3.00
_____ NATURE'S WAY TO NUTRITION & VIBRANT HEALTH *Robert J. Scrutton*   3.00
_____ NEW CARBOHYDRATE DIET COUNTER *Patti Lopez-Pereira*   2.00
_____ REFLEXOLOGY *Dr. Maybelle Segal*   4.00
_____ REFLEXOLOGY FOR GOOD HEALTH *Anna Kaye & Don C. Matchan*   5.00
_____ 30 DAYS TO BEAUTIFUL LEGS *Dr. Marc Selner*   3.00
_____ YOU CAN LEARN TO RELAX *Dr. Samuel Gutwirth*   3.00
_____ YOUR ALLERGY—WHAT TO DO ABOUT IT *Allan Knight, M.D.*   3.00

HOBBIES

_____ BEACHCOMBING FOR BEGINNERS *Norman Hickin*   2.00
_____ BLACKSTONE'S MODERN CARD TRICKS *Harry Blackstone*   5.00
_____ BLACKSTONE'S SECRETS OF MAGIC *Harry Blackstone*   5.00
_____ COIN COLLECTING FOR BEGINNERS *Burton Hobson & Fred Reinfeld*   5.00
_____ ENTERTAINING WITH ESP *Tony 'Doc' Shiels*   2.00
_____ 400 FASCINATING MAGIC TRICKS YOU CAN DO *Howard Thurston*   5.00
_____ HOW I TURN JUNK INTO FUN AND PROFIT *Sari*   3.00
_____ HOW TO WRITE A HIT SONG & SELL IT *Tommy Boyce*   7.00
_____ JUGGLING MADE EASY *Rudolf Dittrich*   3.00
_____ MAGIC FOR ALL AGES *Walter Gibson*   4.00
_____ MAGIC MADE EASY *Byron Wels*   2.00
_____ STAMP COLLECTING FOR BEGINNERS *Burton Hobson*   3.00

HORSE PLAYER'S WINNING GUIDES

_____ BETTING HORSES TO WIN *Les Conklin*   5.00
_____ ELIMINATE THE LOSERS *Bob McKnight*   5.00
_____ HOW TO PICK WINNING HORSES *Bob McKnight*   5.00
_____ HOW TO WIN AT THE RACES *Sam (The Genius) Lewin*   5.00

____ HOW YOU CAN BEAT THE RACES *Jack Kavanaqh*	5.00
____ MAKING MONEY AT THE RACES *David Barr*	5.00
____ PAYDAY AT THE RACES *Les Conklin*	5.00
____ SMART HANDICAPPING MADE EASY *William Bauman*	5.00
____ SUCCESS AT THE HARNESS RACES *Barry Meadow*	5.00
____ WINNING AT THE HARNESS RACES—AN EXPERT'S GUIDE *Nick Cammarano*	5.00

HUMOR

____ HOW TO FLATTEN YOUR TUSH *Coach Marge Reardon*	2.00
____ HOW TO MAKE LOVE TO YOURSELF *Ron Stevens & Joy Grdnic*	3.00
____ JOKE TELLER'S HANDBOOK *Bob Orben*	5.00
____ JOKES FOR ALL OCCASIONS *Al Schock*	5.00
____ 2,000 NEW LAUGHS FOR SPEAKERS *Bob Orben*	5.00
____ 2,500 JOKES TO START 'EM LAUGHING *Bob Orben*	5.00

HYPNOTISM

____ ADVANCED TECHNIQUES OF HYPNOSIS *Melvin Powers*	3.00
____ CHILDBIRTH WITH HYPNOSIS *William S. Kroger, M.D.*	5.00
____ HOW TO SOLVE YOUR SEX PROBLEMS WITH SELF-HYPNOSIS *Frank S. Caprio, M.D.*	5.00
____ HOW TO STOP SMOKING THRU SELF-HYPNOSIS *Leslie M. LeCron*	3.00
____ HOW TO USE AUTO-SUGGESTION EFFECTIVELY *John Duckworth*	3.00
____ HOW YOU CAN BOWL BETTER USING SELF-HYPNOSIS *Jack Heise*	4.00
____ HOW YOU CAN PLAY BETTER GOLF USING SELF-HYPNOSIS *Jack Heise*	3.00
____ HYPNOSIS AND SELF-HYPNOSIS *Bernard Hollander, M.D.*	5.00
____ HYPNOTISM *(Originally published in 1893) Carl Sextus*	5.00
____ HYPNOTISM & PSYCHIC PHENOMENA *Simeon Edmunds*	4.00
____ HYPNOTISM MADE EASY *Dr. Ralph Winn*	5.00
____ HYPNOTISM MADE PRACTICAL *Louis Orton*	5.00
____ HYPNOTISM REVEALED *Melvin Powers*	3.00
____ HYPNOTISM TODAY *Leslie LeCron and Jean Bordeaux, Ph.D.*	5.00
____ MODERN HYPNOSIS *Lesley Kuhn & Salvatore Russo, Ph.D.*	5.00
____ NEW CONCEPTS OF HYPNOSIS *Bernard C. Gindes, M.D.*	7.00
____ NEW SELF-HYPNOSIS *Paul Adams*	7.00
____ POST-HYPNOTIC INSTRUCTIONS—SUGGESTIONS FOR THERAPY *Arnold Furst*	5.00
____ PRACTICAL GUIDE TO SELF-HYPNOSIS *Melvin Powers*	3.00
____ PRACTICAL HYPNOTISM *Philip Magonet, M.D.*	3.00
____ SECRETS OF HYPNOTISM *S. J. Van Pelt, M.D.*	5.00
____ SELF-HYPNOSIS—A CONDITIONED-RESPONSE TECHNIQUE *Laurence Sparks*	7.00
____ SELF-HYPNOSIS—ITS THEORY, TECHNIQUE & APPLICATION *Melvin Powers*	3.00
____ THERAPY THROUGH HYPNOSIS *Edited by Raphael H. Rhodes*	5.00

JUDAICA

____ SERVICE OF THE HEART *Evelyn Garfiel, Ph.D.*	7.00
____ STORY OF ISRAEL IN COINS *Jean & Maurice Gould*	2.00
____ STORY OF ISRAEL IN STAMPS *Maxim & Gabriel Shamir*	1.00
____ TONGUE OF THE PROPHETS *Robert St. John*	7.00

JUST FOR WOMEN

____ COSMOPOLITAN'S GUIDE TO MARVELOUS MEN Foreword by *Helen Gurley Brown*	3.00
____ COSMOPOLITAN'S HANG-UP HANDBOOK Foreword by *Helen Gurley Brown*	4.00
____ COSMOPOLITAN'S LOVE BOOK—A GUIDE TO ECSTASY IN BED	7.00
____ COSMOPOLITAN'S NEW ETIQUETTE GUIDE Foreword by *Helen Gurley Brown*	4.00
____ I AM A COMPLEAT WOMAN *Doris Hagopian & Karen O'Connor Sweeney*	3.00
____ JUST FOR WOMEN—A GUIDE TO THE FEMALE BODY *Richard E. Sand, M.D.*	5.00
____ NEW APPROACHES TO SEX IN MARRIAGE *John E. Eichenlaub, M.D.*	3.00
____ SEXUALLY ADEQUATE FEMALE *Frank S. Caprio, M.D.*	3.00
____ SEXUALLY FULFILLED WOMAN *Dr. Rachel Copelan*	5.00
____ YOUR FIRST YEAR OF MARRIAGE *Dr. Tom McGinnis*	3.00

MARRIAGE, SEX & PARENTHOOD

____ ABILITY TO LOVE *Dr. Allan Fromme*	7.00
____ GUIDE TO SUCCESSFUL MARRIAGE *Drs. Albert Ellis & Robert Harper*	7.00

____ HOW TO RAISE AN EMOTIONALLY HEALTHY, HAPPY CHILD *Albert Ellis, Ph.D.*	7.00
____ PARENT SURVIVAL TRAINING *Marvin Silverman, Ed.D. & David Lustig, Ph.D.*	10.00
____ SEX WITHOUT GUILT *Albert Ellis, Ph.D.*	5.00
____ SEXUALLY ADEQUATE MALE *Frank S. Caprio, M.D.*	3.00
____ SEXUALLY FULFILLED MAN *Dr. Rachel Copelan*	5.00
____ STAYING IN LOVE *Dr. Norton F. Kristy*	7.00

MELVIN POWERS' MAIL ORDER LIBRARY

____ HOW TO GET RICH IN MAIL ORDER *Melvin Powers*	20.00
____ HOW TO WRITE A GOOD ADVERTISEMENT *Victor O. Schwab*	20.00
____ MAIL ORDER MADE EASY *J. Frank Brumbaugh*	20.00

METAPHYSICS & OCCULT

____ BOOK OF TALISMANS, AMULETS & ZODIACAL GEMS *William Pavitt*	7.00
____ CONCENTRATION—A GUIDE TO MENTAL MASTERY *Mouni Sadhu*	5.00
____ EXTRA-TERRESTRIAL INTELLIGENCE—THE FIRST ENCOUNTER	6.00
____ FORTUNE TELLING WITH CARDS *P. Foli*	5.00
____ HOW TO INTERPRET DREAMS, OMENS & FORTUNE TELLING SIGNS *Gettings*	5.00
____ HOW TO UNDERSTAND YOUR DREAMS *Geoffrey A. Dudley*	5.00
____ IN DAYS OF GREAT PEACE *Mouni Sadhu*	3.00
____ LSD—THE AGE OF MIND *Bernard Roseman*	2.00
____ MAGICIAN—HIS TRAINING AND WORK *W. E. Butler*	5.00
____ MEDITATION *Mouni Sadhu*	7.00
____ MODERN NUMEROLOGY *Morris C. Goodman*	5.00
____ NUMEROLOGY—ITS FACTS AND SECRETS *Ariel Yvon Taylor*	5.00
____ NUMEROLOGY MADE EASY *W. Mykian*	5.00
____ PALMISTRY MADE EASY *Fred Gettings*	5.00
____ PALMISTRY MADE PRACTICAL *Elizabeth Daniels Squire*	5.00
____ PALMISTRY SECRETS REVEALED *Henry Frith*	4.00
____ PROPHECY IN OUR TIME *Martin Ebon*	2.50
____ SUPERSTITION—ARE YOU SUPERSTITIOUS? *Eric Maple*	2.00
____ TAROT *Mouni Sadhu*	10.00
____ TAROT OF THE BOHEMIANS *Papus*	7.00
____ WAYS TO SELF-REALIZATION *Mouni Sadhu*	7.00
____ WITCHCRAFT, MAGIC & OCCULTISM—A FASCINATING HISTORY *W. B. Crow*	7.00
____ WITCHCRAFT—THE SIXTH SENSE *Justine Glass*	7.00
____ WORLD OF PSYCHIC RESEARCH *Hereward Carrington*	2.00

SELF-HELP & INSPIRATIONAL

____ CHARISMA—HOW TO GET "THAT SPECIAL MAGIC" *Marcia Grad*	7.00
____ DAILY POWER FOR JOYFUL LIVING *Dr. Donald Curtis*	5.00
____ DYNAMIC THINKING *Melvin Powers*	5.00
____ GREATEST POWER IN THE UNIVERSE *U. S. Andersen*	7.00
____ GROW RICH WHILE YOU SLEEP *Ben Sweetland*	7.00
____ GROWTH THROUGH REASON *Albert Ellis, Ph.D.*	7.00
____ GUIDE TO PERSONAL HAPPINESS *Albert Ellis, Ph.D. & Irving Becker, Ed.D.*	7.00
____ HANDWRITING ANALYSIS MADE EASY *John Marley*	5.00
____ HANDWRITING TELLS *Nadya Olyanova*	7.00
____ HOW TO ATTRACT GOOD LUCK *A.H.Z. Carr*	7.00
____ HOW TO BE GREAT *Dr. Donald Curtis*	5.00
____ HOW TO DEVELOP A WINNING PERSONALITY *Martin Panzer*	5.00
____ HOW TO DEVELOP AN EXCEPTIONAL MEMORY *Young & Gibson*	5.00
____ HOW TO LIVE WITH A NEUROTIC *Albert Ellis, Ph.D.*	5.00
____ HOW TO OVERCOME YOUR FEARS *M. P. Leahy, M.D.*	3.00
____ HOW TO SUCCEED *Brian Adams*	7.00
____ HUMAN PROBLEMS & HOW TO SOLVE THEM *Dr. Donald Curtis*	5.00
____ I CAN *Ben Sweetland*	7.00
____ I WILL *Ben Sweetland*	3.00
____ KNIGHT IN THE RUSTY ARMOR *Robert Fisher*	10.00
____ LEFT-HANDED PEOPLE *Michael Barsley*	5.00
____ MAGIC IN YOUR MIND *U.S. Andersen*	7.00

____ MAGIC OF THINKING BIG *Dr. David J. Schwartz*		3.00
____ MAGIC OF THINKING SUCCESS *Dr. David J. Schwartz*		7.00
____ MAGIC POWER OF YOUR MIND *Walter M. Germain*		7.00
____ MENTAL POWER THROUGH SLEEP SUGGESTION *Melvin Powers*		3.00
____ NEVER UNDERESTIMATE THE SELLING POWER OF A WOMAN *Dottie Walters*		7.00
____ NEW GUIDE TO RATIONAL LIVING *Albert Ellis, Ph.D. & R. Harper, Ph.D.*		7.00
____ PSYCHO-CYBERNETICS *Maxwell Maltz, M.D.*		7.00
____ PSYCHOLOGY OF HANDWRITING *Nadya Olyanova*		7.00
____ SALES CYBERNETICS *Brian Adams*		7.00
____ SCIENCE OF MIND IN DAILY LIVING *Dr. Donald Curtis*		7.00
____ SECRET OF SECRETS *U.S. Andersen*		7.00
____ SECRET POWER OF THE PYRAMIDS *U. S. Andersen*		7.00
____ SELF-THERAPY FOR THE STUTTERER *Malcolm Frazer*		3.00
____ SUCCESS-CYBERNETICS *U. S. Andersen*		7.00
____ 10 DAYS TO A GREAT NEW LIFE *William E. Edwards*		3.00
____ THINK AND GROW RICH *Napoleon Hill*		7.00
____ THINK YOUR WAY TO SUCCESS *Dr. Lew Losoncy*		5.00
____ THREE MAGIC WORDS *U. S. Andersen*		7.00
____ TREASURY OF COMFORT *Edited by Rabbi Sidney Greenberg*		7.00
____ TREASURY OF THE ART OF LIVING *Sidney S. Greenberg*		7.00
____ WHAT YOUR HANDWRITING REVEALS *Albert E. Hughes*		3.00
____ YOUR SUBCONSCIOUS POWER *Charles M. Simmons*		7.00
____ YOUR THOUGHTS CAN CHANGE YOUR LIFE *Dr. Donald Curtis*		7.00

SPORTS

____ BICYCLING FOR FUN AND GOOD HEALTH *Kenneth E. Luther*		2.00
____ BILLIARDS—POCKET • CAROM • THREE CUSION *Clive Cottingham, Jr.*		5.00
____ CAMPING-OUT—101 IDEAS & ACTIVITIES *Bruno Knobel*		2.00
____ COMPLETE GUIDE TO FISHING *Vlad Evanoff*		2.00
____ HOW TO IMPROVE YOUR RACQUETBALL *Lubarsky, Kaufman & Scagnetti*		5.00
____ HOW TO WIN AT POCKET BILLIARDS *Edward D. Knuchell*		5.00
____ JOY OF WALKING *Jack Scagnetti*		3.00
____ LEARNING & TEACHING SOCCER SKILLS *Eric Worthington*		3.00
____ MOTORCYCLING FOR BEGINNERS *I.G. Edmonds*		3.00
____ RACQUETBALL FOR WOMEN *Toni Hudson, Jack Scagnetti & Vince Rondone*		3.00
____ RACQUETBALL MADE EASY *Steve Lubarsky, Rod Delson & Jack Scagnetti*		5.00
____ SECRET OF BOWLING STRIKES *Dawson Taylor*		5.00
____ SECRET OF PERFECT PUTTING *Horton Smith & Dawson Taylor*		5.00
____ SOCCER—THE GAME & HOW TO PLAY IT *Gary Rosenthal*		5.00
____ STARTING SOCCER *Edward F. Dolan, Jr.*		5.00

TENNIS LOVER'S LIBRARY

____ BEGINNER'S GUIDE TO WINNING TENNIS *Helen Hull Jacobs*		2.00
____ HOW TO BEAT BETTER TENNIS PLAYERS *Loring Fiske*		4.00
____ HOW TO IMPROVE YOUR TENNIS—STYLE, STRATEGY & ANALYSIS *C. Wilson*		2.00
____ PSYCH YOURSELF TO BETTER TENNIS *Dr. Walter A. Luszki*		2.00
____ TENNIS FOR BEGINNERS *Dr. H. A. Murray*		2.00
____ TENNIS MADE EASY *Joel Brecheen*		5.00
____ WEEKEND TENNIS—HOW TO HAVE FUN & WIN AT THE SAME TIME *Bill Talbert*		3.00
____ WINNING WITH PERCENTAGE TENNIS—SMART STRATEGY *Jack Lowe*		2.00

WILSHIRE PET LIBRARY

____ DOG OBEDIENCE TRAINING *Gust Kessopulos*		5.00
____ DOG TRAINING MADE EASY & FUN *John W. Kellogg*		5.00
____ HOW TO BRING UP YOUR PET DOG *Kurt Unkelbach*		2.00
____ HOW TO RAISE & TRAIN YOUR PUPPY *Jeff Griffen*		5.00

The books listed above can be obtained from your book dealer or directly from Melvin Powers. When ordering, please remit $1.00 postage for the first book and 50¢ for each additional book.

Melvin Powers
12015 Sherman Road, No. Hollywood, California 91605

HOW TO GET RICH IN MAIL ORDER
by Melvin Powers

Contents:
1. How to Develop Your Mail Order Expertise 2. How to Find a Unique Product or Service to Sell 3. How to Make Money with Classified Ads 4. How to Make Money with Display Ads 5. The Unlimited Potential for Making Money with Direct Mail 6. How to Copycat Successful Mail Order Operations 7. How I Created A Best Seller Using the Copycat Technique 8. How to Start and Run a Profitable Mail Order, Special Interest Book or Record Business 9. I Enjoy Selling Books by Mail—Some of My Successful and Not-So-Successful Ads and Direct Mail Circulars 10. Five of My Most Successful Direct Mail Pieces That Sold and Are Still Selling Millions of Dollars Worth of Books 11. Melvin Powers' Mail Order Success Strategy—Follow It and You'll Become a Millionaire 12. How to Sell Your Products to Mail Order Companies, Retail Outlets, Jobbers, and Fund Raisers for Maximum Distribution and Profits 13. How to Get Free Display Ads and Publicity That Can Put You on the Road to Riches 14. How to Make Your Advertising Copy Sizzle to Make You Wealthy 15. Questions and Answers to Help You Get Started Making Money in Your Own Mail Order Business 16. A Personal Word from Melvin Powers   **8½" x 11" — 352 Pages . . . $21 postpaid**

HOW TO SELF-PUBLISH YOUR BOOK AND HAVE THE FUN AND EXCITEMENT OF BEING A BEST-SELLING AUTHOR
by Melvin Powers

An expert's step-by-step guide to marketing your book successfully

176 Pages . . . $11.00 postpaid

A NEW GUIDE TO RATIONAL LIVING
by Albert Ellis, Ph.D. & Robert A. Harper, Ph.D.

Contents:
1. How Far Can You Go With Self-Analysis? 2. You Feel the Way You Think 3. Feeling Well by Thinking Straight 4. How You Create Your Feelings 5. Thinking Yourself Out of Emotional Disturbances 6. Recognizing and Attacking Neurotic Behavior 7. Overcoming the Influences of the Past 8. Does Reason Always Prove Reasonable? 9. Refusing to Feel Desperately Unhappy 10. Tackling Dire Needs for Approval 11. Eradicating Dire Fears of Failure 12. How to Stop Blaming and Start Living 13. How to Feel Undepressed though Frustrated 14. Controlling Your Own Destiny 15. Conquering Anxiety

256 Pages . . . $3.50 postpaid

PSYCHO-CYBERNETICS
A New Technique for Using Your Subconscious Power
by Maxwell Maltz, M.D., F.I.C.S.

Contents:
1. The Self Image: Your Key to a Better Life 2. Discovering the Success Mechanism Within You 3. Imagination—The First Key to Your Success Mechanism 4. Dehypnotize Yourself from False Beliefs 5. How to Utilize the Power of Rational Thinking 6. Relax and Let Your Success Mechanism Work for You 7. You Can Acquire the Habit of Happiness 8. Ingredients of the Success-Type Personality and How to Acquire Them 9. The Failure Mechanism: How to Make It Work For You Instead of Against You 10. How to Remove Emotional Scars, or How to Give Yourself an Emotional Face Lift 11. How to Unlock Your Real Personality 12. Do-It-Yourself Tranquilizers   **288 Pages . . . $5.50 postpaid**

A PRACTICAL GUIDE TO SELF-HYPNOSIS
by Melvin Powers

Contents:
1. What You Should Know About Self-Hypnosis 2. What About the Dangers of Hypnosis? 3. Is Hypnosis the Answer? 4. How Does Self-Hypnosis Work? 5. How to Arouse Yourself from the Self-Hypnotic State 6. How to Attain Self-Hypnosis 7. Deepening the Self-Hypnotic State 8. What You Should Know About Becoming an Excellent Subject 9. Techniques for Reaching the Somnambulistic State 10. A New Approach to Self-Hypnosis When All Else Fails 11. Psychological Aids and Their Function 12. The Nature of Hypnosis 13. Practical Applications of Self-Hypnosis   **128 Pages . . . $3.50 postpaid**

The books listed above can be obtained from your book dealer or directly from Melvin Powers.

Melvin Powers
12015 Sherman Road, No. Hollywood, California 91605